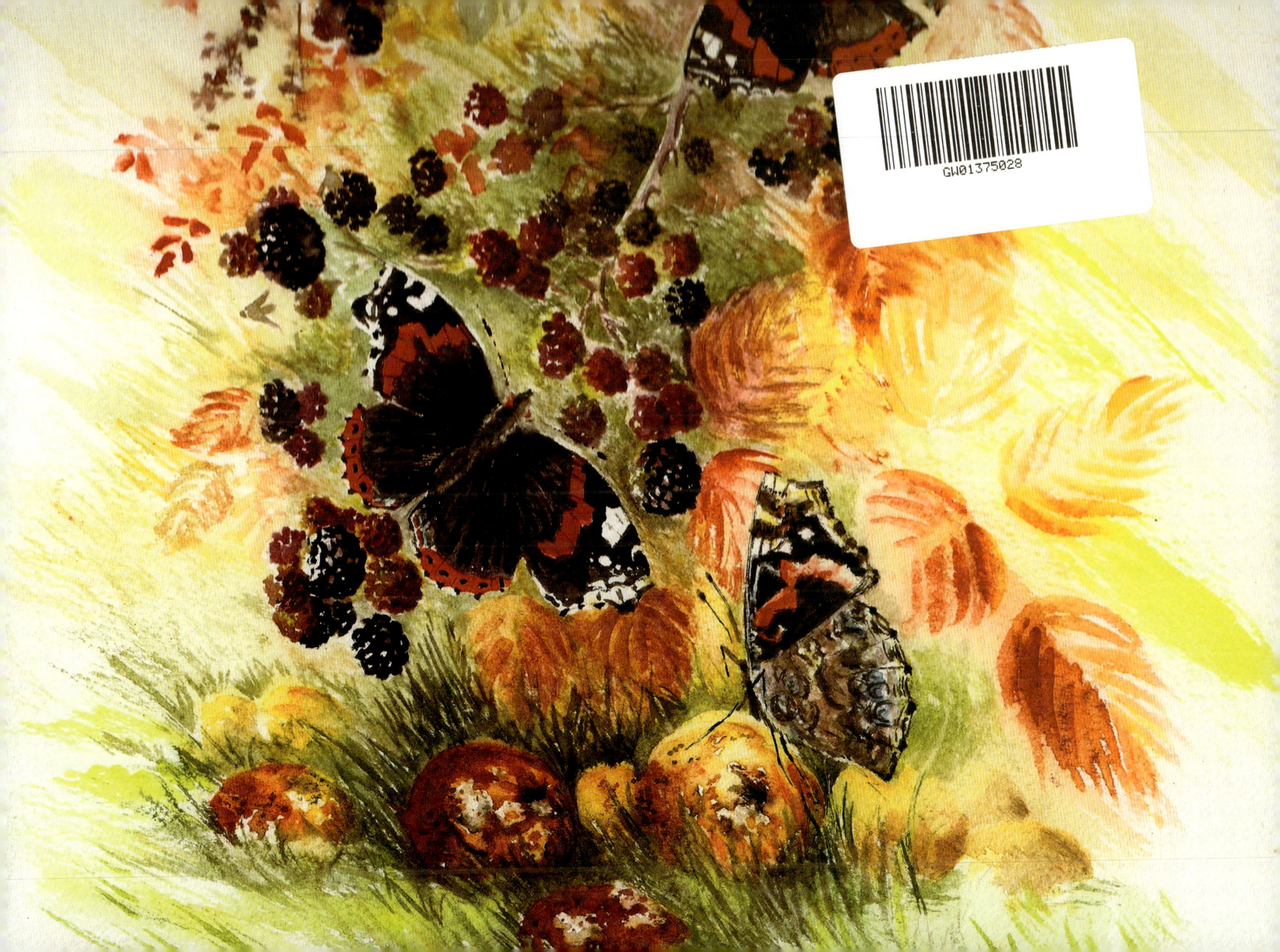

ACKNOWLEDGEMENTS

Thanks to Jane Hince for typing the original script; my neighbours, the two Js, for final proofreading; Sarah and Joyce at Inkwell Media – and finally to my family for their patience amidst unwashed shirts and uncooked dinners during the creation of this book.

Little Green Shoots

TALES FROM A COTSWOLD TEACHER

ILLUSTRATED BY JENNY HENDERSON

© Illustrations and text 2010: Jenny Henderson
© Design and compilation: Inkwell Media Limited

No part of this publication may be reproduced, stored in or introduced into a retrieval system, or transmitted, in any form or by any means (electronic, mechanical, photocopying, recording or otherwise) without prior written permission of Jenny Henderson and Inkwell Media Limited.

Designed and produced by
Inkwell Media Limited
274 Richmond Road
London E8 3QW
Tel: 0207 637 1787 (London) or
07971 554112 (Gloucestershire)

ISBN 978-0-9560859-6-2

HOW TO ORDER PRINTS

All the illustrations in this book are available to purchase as prints. Please refer to the list on Page 83 (and contact me at **jennys.art@hotmail.co.uk** so I can discuss your order personally – Jenny Henderson).

inkwell

media is a publishing company that creates affordable custom-made books and calendars for schools and organisations – or for individual authors and artists. We specialise in short print-runs.

If you are interested in publishing a book of short stories, poetry or recipes – or in creating a book for your community or for fundraising – please contact us on the numbers above or through our website (**www.inkwellmedia.co.uk**).

A Little Disclaimer

These tales are a pudding-mix of true little incidents, which happened after I moved to the Cotswolds in the 1970s and began teaching. To attempt anonymity, their history has been condensed into three school terms and their geography combined into one place. The characters are not individuals but ingredients which have been blended, baked and sliced into slabs of multi-coloured fruit-cake where the nuts and the cherries can hopefully still be seen.

The illustrations are mostly Cotswold scenes, not necessarily connected to the tales and others are mainly muddled memories. Any faces are impressions of the illustrator's children.

Profits from book sales will allow a donation to be made to rural youth and home nursing charities.

A Little Foreword

When my eldest child had just started school, armed with enthusiasm at the beginning of her adventures in education, I took in small sack of wheat grains. Her teacher stared vacantly back at me,

"We didn't ask for that," she stated and handed it back.
I recalled my own teaching days. The crisp Autumn Term was an embodiment of seeds and harvest. Children brought in home-grown apples and pumpkins to cut open and draw, conkers and cob-nuts to sort and count, russet leaves to press and print – and I always took in a bag of wheat grains. Each child was given 100 grains. They planted, watered and nurtured the grains until the little green shoots popped their dewdrop tips out of the soil.

"I've got five Miss!"

"I've got twenty one!"

"All hundred of mine have grown Miss!" and so they unwittingly learnt about percentages.

"Let's see how many will grow if we don't water them, or if we keep them in the dark," I would suggest.

"Mine went all yellow Miss, – shall I paint them green?"

"Mine never grew at all Miss. Why not?"

"Mine are best. Mine were nearest the heater," continued the science lesson.

Just in those few intervening years, teaching had changed. They didn't want those little green shoots sprouting in their orderly, controlled classrooms.

I miss those little green shoots.

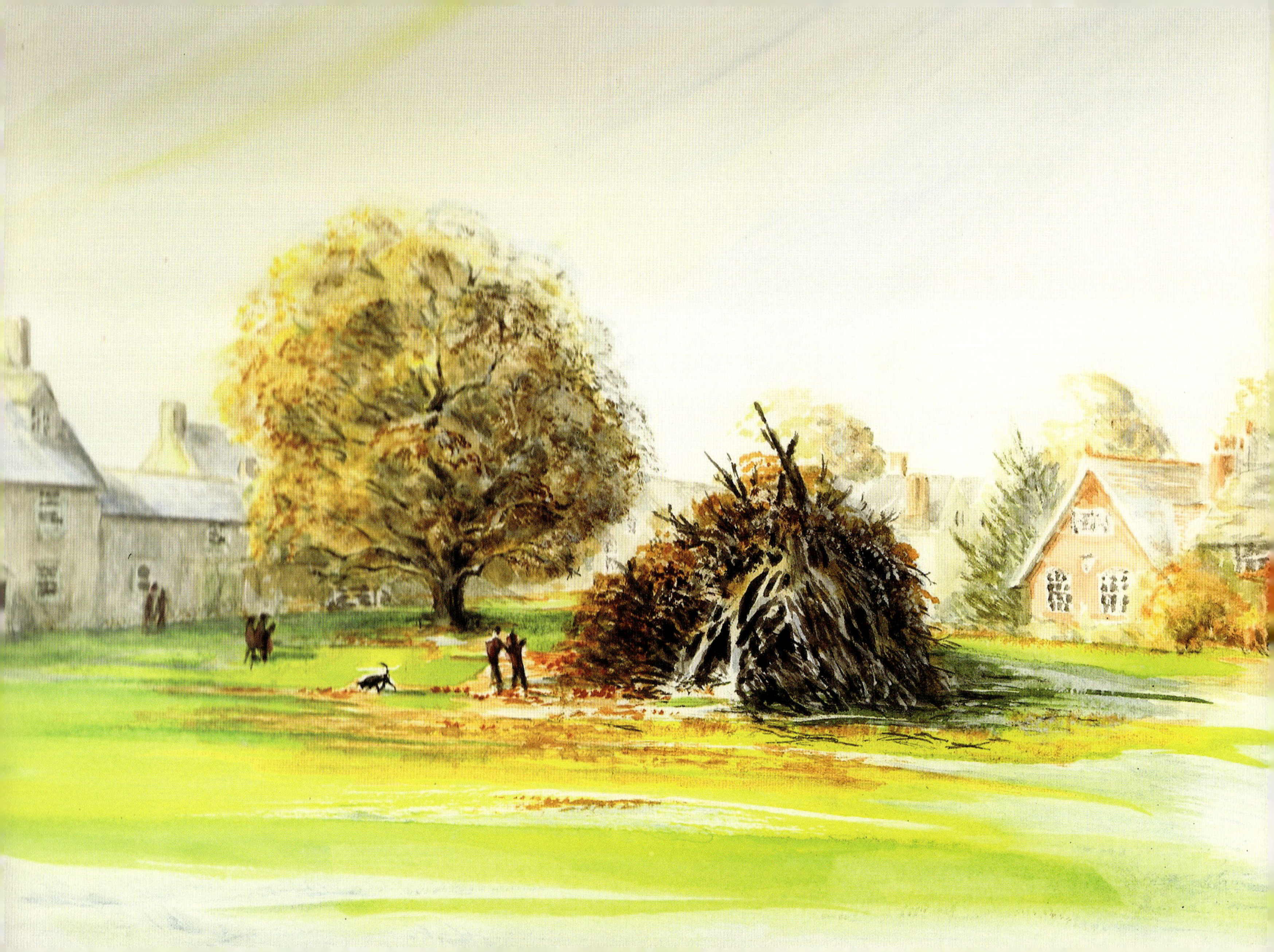

Contents

AUTUMN TERM

First Steps	9
Strawberry Sponge with Pink Custard	10
Mini-troubles	13
'Woof'	15
Over the Wall	16
Home Sweet Home	17
Welcome In the New	21
Funetix and Eemerjunt Ryting	24
Grammar Rules OK	25
Dressed for Christmas	29

SPRING TERM

I'm in Charge	32
The Scourge of the Ice Breaker	35
Smile Please	36
A Mad Menagerie	38
Something Scary in the Scullery	40
On the Topic of Time	42
There's None so Queer as Folk	42
We Are ALL Special	43
A Bit of Helpful Advice	45
'Is he Dyslexic?' 'No he Just Can't Read.'	48
Lost for Words	49
Walk on ... Walk on ...	51
Eggs is Eggs	54

SUMMER TERM

Cricket is Cricket	57
Playground Games	62
A Fallen Idol	63
Pastures New	64
Dancing Queen	66
Tigger was Very Bouncy	68
Hooper's Hedgerow	69
The Giant Yellow Monster	70
You Can't Win them All	72
A Question of Trust	74
Matters of Privacy	76

POSTSCRIPT

The Beginning of the End	79

Autumn Term

First Steps

My first day in my first teaching job. Scary. I was greeted in the playground by a very skippy girl in a brown dress, matching her brown curls and dark brown eyes. She grabbed my arm with two skinny hands.

"What's your name Miss, mine's Tina?" she beamed but when she saw other girls approaching she withdrew and melted silently into the background.

"I like your dress Miss."

"Your hair's nice," the others flattered, clinging to my arms. A few boys walked over to the car I'd just parked – an old 1960 Mini – and dismissed it, dismissed me and continued their game.

My village school had four classes, two in the ancient stone building and two overflowing into the temporary classrooms which had been temporary for well over ten years. Between them was a large playground with climbing frames and a huge hollow elm tree stump made into a Wendy house. Besides this, through a farm gate and surrounded by a dry-stone wall, was a little paddock with a pond where a few ducks and chickens puddled and scratched. A cacophony of homemade hutches lined the wall, in which children were allowed to keep their pet rabbits and guinea-pigs. Next to the paddock was a small outdoor swimming pool, courtesy of the Friends of the School.

Our teaching college was apt to describe children in small rural schools as 'socially deprived'. I soon learnt that this was not the case. They had no computers, PlayStations or mobile phones then but had more freedom to play, always outside, in various mixed groups, older ones helping little ones. There were also organised clubs for those who chose such as Cubs, Brownies and Guides. A few went to ballet classes, music lessons or horse-riding and others could join in the senior cricket or football clubs – most of the time though, they just played 'out '.

A village hall provided the venue for Youth Club, Young Farmers, whist drives, bingo, jumble sales, dances and parties. One or two families had never even left the village but for those who wanted there were buses to towns and trains all the way to London.

It was a bustling working village. From stone moss-laden cottages, blue-slated Victorian houses and modern dwellings the occupants drove or walked to work locally in shops, farms, hotels or factories. The elderly or retired popped faces out of rose-clad windows to watch the children on their way to school. Not everyone 'got on', but they all knew each other and if they knew they didn't 'get on', they just didn't speak. It worked.

Strawberry Sponge with Pink Custard

My first morning had gone reasonably well. I had learnt which mugs not to use in the staff room and which chairs not to sit in. I got most of the children's names right and managed to get Tina to finally release her vice-like grip on my arm. There was a good general 'working hum' in the classroom – a mixture of work and holiday gossip, acceptable on a first day – and apart from Tina, no tears.

Suddenly the playground door burst open and in walked a huge over-laden tray of plates and cutlery accompanied by a white-aproned cook.

"Mornin' Miss!" she beamed.

This appeared to be the signal for absolute mayhem as books were slammed shut, pencils and crayons thrown in pots, pencils and crayons missing pots, and children rushing everywhere. Most of the children had dived into the Home Corner where pouffes and cushions hurtled through the air and a few remaining children began rearranging my carefully arranged tables. They dragged them noisily across the floor like a dozen double-basses. Accompanying this was the percussion section, throwing cutlery onto the tables.

"It's 15 minutes story-time before lunch Miss," prompted the cook coming to my rescue as she scuttled back to the kitchen hut for spoons, ladles, carrots, greens and mince. After this initial shock, I found these 15 gifted minutes a great time for learning spellings, tables or phonics with the added incentive of 'who's going to be first for dinner?' This worked well – unless it was salad.

Our school meals were wholesome and healthy. Blackberry pies, rhubarb crumbles, Eve's pudding, pink custard, brown stew, carrots and even greens were eaten with relish. All the food was fresh, local and lovingly prepared and cooked by Mrs Spooner and her assistant in her tiny wooden hut across the playground.

After one morning playtime some of the children came back to class in tears.

"There's a new lady in the kitchen hut."

"She's cross."

"She won't cut up our oranges for us," Timmy protested, picking away unsuccessfully at the peel.

"She told us to go away," whimpered Tina, bottom lip trembling.

The full story emerged later on. The kitchen had been visited by a 'School Meals Advisor'. The advisor first advised Mrs Spooner that if she was really going to serve cabbage to children she should add green colouring to make it more attractive. She then asked about the main course accompanying the cabbage.

"Garden Casserole," Mrs Spooner proudly announced "with local beef from 'down the hill' and vegetables from the garden 'up the hill' – all fresh," she said folding her arms with satisfaction.

"Stew?" the advisor sneered, "you can't serve STEW to today's children. They want modern foods like pizzas – I'll show you!" she said wiping all the vegetables off the chopping boards and rolling out a grey pre-prepared dough which she wiped with ketchup, adding floppy square dollops of plastic cheese.

"Now, make 25 of these and cut into quarters. There's ice-cream for dessert in my cool-box."

Mrs Spooner slowly unfolded her arms, took off her hat and apron and placed them neatly on the table. She then majestically marched out of the kitchen retorting,

"If you want pizzas, you can make them yourself!"

Her assistant hovered nervously over the pizza dough for just a second – then she dispensed with her hat and apron too, following Mrs Spooner out, both relating the event house after house all their way home. A few curious onlookers gathered outside the school at lunchtime in eager anticipation of a dramatic finale.

By lunchtime, dinner had not arrived. The children had set the tables and glumly waited in silence. Eventually the large door squeaked open and a flour-dusted School Meals Advisor appeared carrying a tray of 100 tiny pizza quarters. These were devoured rapidly by 100 hungry children. The advisor seemed smugly delighted until the boys asked where the main course was. She returned with the pudding, 100 tiny portions of bright pink ice-cream rolled up in pieces of cardboard.

"Ugh! It's inside a toilet roll!" roared one of the boys.

Needless to say, after that, only the wafer-thin wafers were consumed and 100 dejected children went hungrily out to play.

Horror stories began to circulate around the village of starvation, tummy-aches and tears. Several parents demanded their dinner-money back and vowed to take their children home for lunch. Impromptu meetings were held in village parlours and front rooms and Mrs Spooner was implored to withdraw her resignation. Meanwhile the school kitchen remained closed and the children went home for lunch, rather disrupting our lunch-time clubs. Eventually Mrs Spooner was persuaded to come back,

"But on MY terms!" she finger-wagged.

They were good terms too for all of us. We saw no more meals advisors but did see a Health Inspector which resulted in a brand new school kitchen being built, bringing an end to custard and carrot remains on my classroom tables.

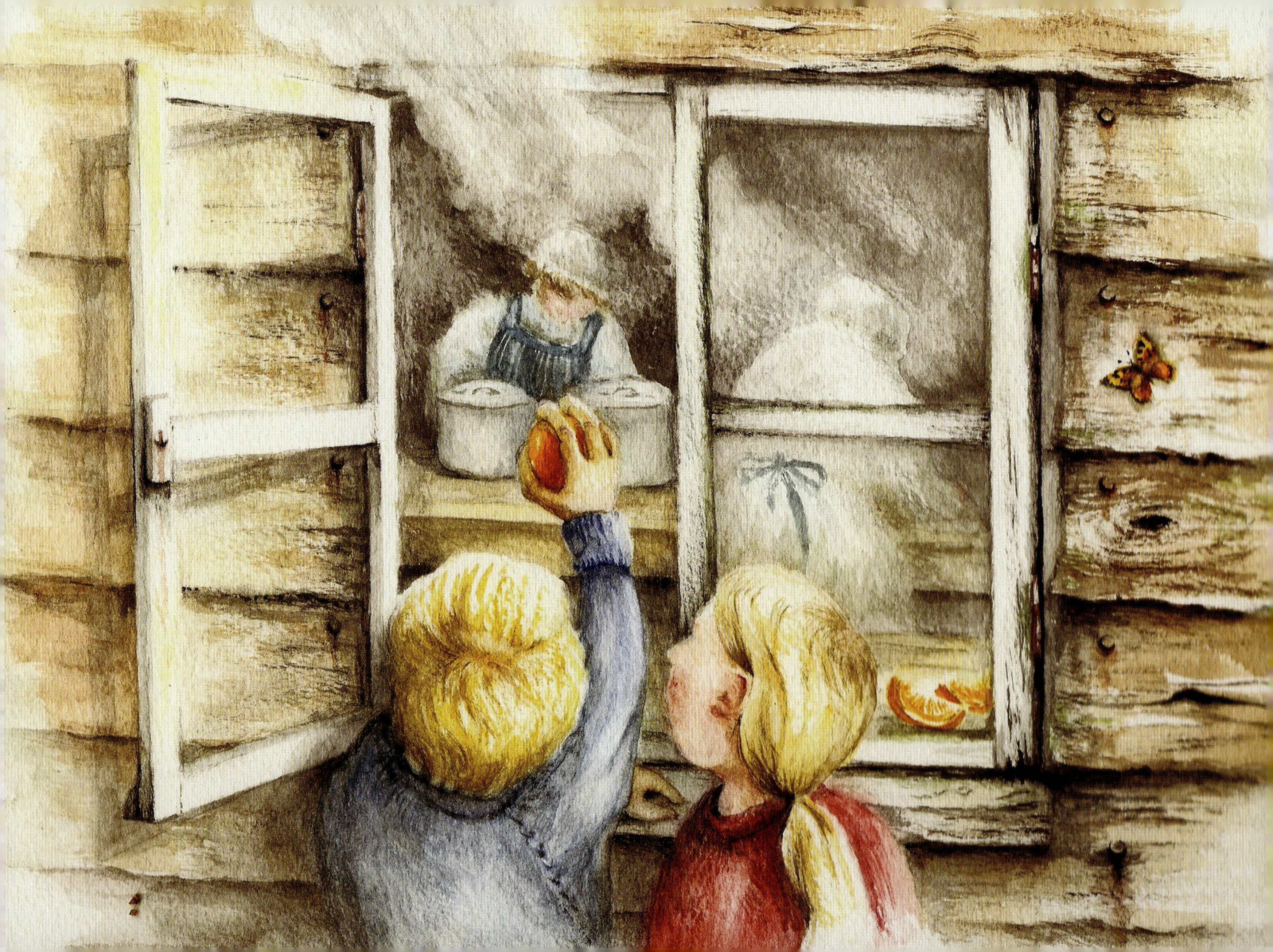

Mini-troubles

It took a while to get to know the 'ways of the village'. One evening my beloved little blue Mini refused to start. The village garage was run by one of the older junior's dads so the following day I asked Rory to ask his dad if he would pick it up and repair it.

"It's a blue Morris Mini parked outside the school next to where the milk float parks. I think it's the starter motor," I explained handing over the Morris keys. It was still there the following day so I asked Rory if there was a problem.

"Yes Miss. Me dad couldn't find it. You said it were an Austin Mini an' there weren't no Austin there."

"No, I said a 'Morris Mini'. Would he collect my MORRIS Mini then please."

The car was collected and repaired but not returned and I was asked to go and collect it. Upon arrival at the garage I faced an amused audience of mechanics – Rory, Rory's friends and his dad.

"What made you think it were the starter motor?"

"Well – it wouldn't start," I answered defiantly.

"Well – it weren't the starter motor," Rory's dad chuckled .

"No?"

"What fuel did you put in it lass?"

"3-star petrol."

There was general all-round laughter now.

"Not Gold Top pintas then?"

I looked puzzled.

"The petrol tank was full of milk!" he roared and general guffawing ensued.

I related the story in the staffroom the next day.

"Your initial mistake" explained the Head, was to *tell them* what you thought was wrong. *They* like to tell you! That's why Rory tried to infer you didn't know the make of your own car."

"And the second mistake?" I ventured,

"Ah. That would be parking your car by the milk-float on Youth Club night."

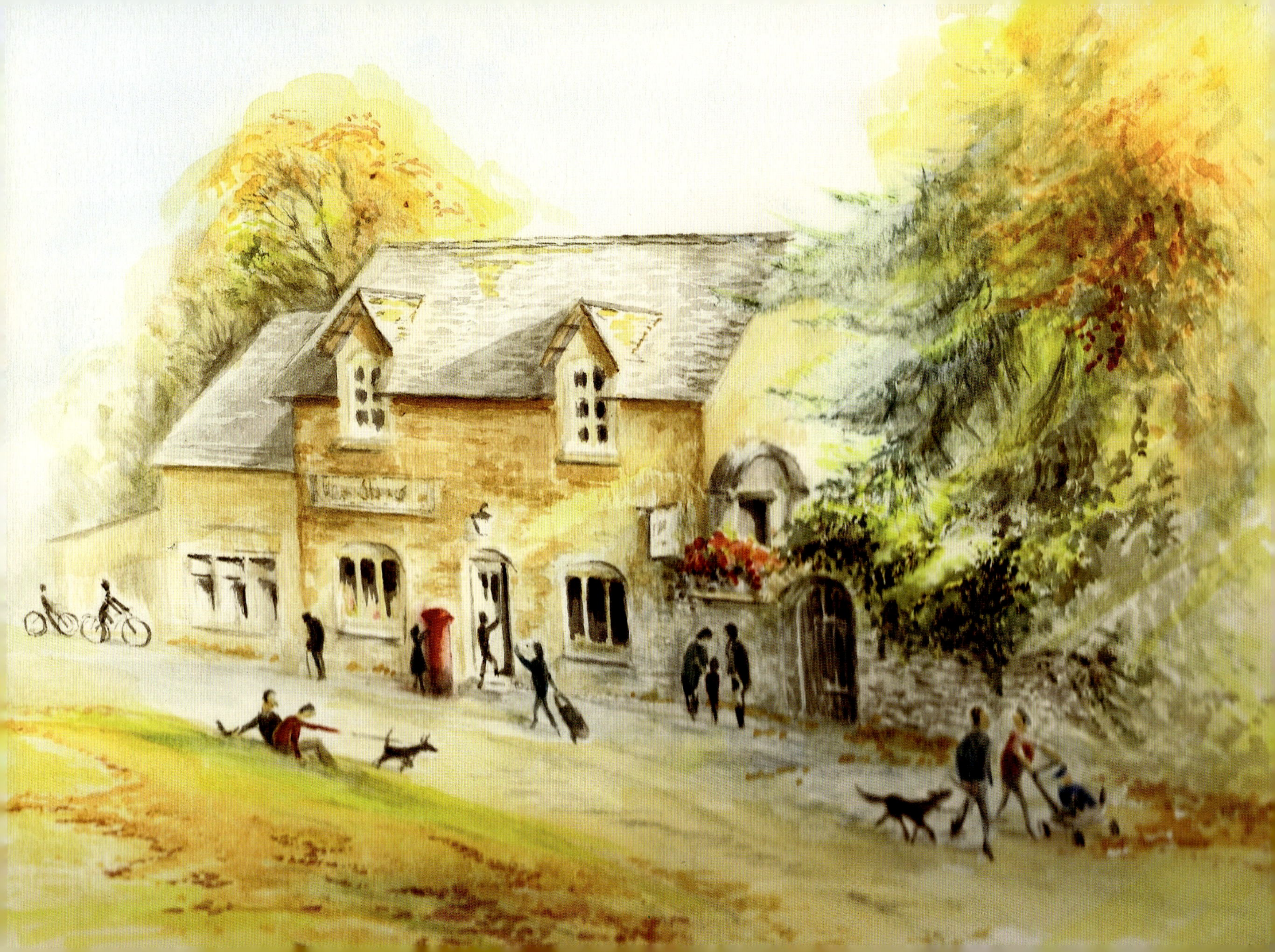

'Woof'

Readers with classic car tendencies will know the significance of my little Mini. If my other readers will allow a short nerdy interlude (go and make a cuppa) I will describe its little mid-life crisis.

Mine was one of the earliest Minis with hollow doors and pull-down wire door-openers. The rest of the interior had lots of useful hollow spaces too, the only exception being the large circular speedo centre dashboard (or lack of dashboard). The colour was a very dignified Cambridge Blue and I recall matching seats but my nerdy friends assure me they must have been red. It had flat chrome wheel hubs, no wing mirrors to my memory and I think the windows had a sliding mechanism.

Its tiny 850cc engine took it regularly on my 200-mile cross-country journey home, humming happily along at 60mph and needing only one drink on its half way coffee-break. It had been in our family since its birth and was much loved. Its name was Woof (after its registration letters, not its speed).

One day Woof went for its annual medical check.

"Sills 've gone," the mechanic said gravely shaking his head, "once sills 've gone it's haddit."

I looked sorrowfully inside the bonnet wondering where the sills were.

"I knows someone 'oo might buy it off you though," he piped up cheerfully.

So I sold it to a lad in the village whose dad thought he could 'do it up' for him. It turned out that his father had some working knowledge of Minis being employed at British Leyland and sure enough the offending sills were skilfully patched, plated and welded like new. His son was soon learning to drive in it, trundling around the country lanes.

Several years later Woof was still alive. Friends had spotted it bombing around Cowley presumably surrounded by hundreds of surplus spare parts and hundreds of knowledgeable, surplus spare hands.

Readers still with me at this juncture will probably know that if I'd kept my beloved £100 classic Mini it would now be worth several multiples of that figure.

Over the Wall

My classroom was in the old part of the school next to the reception teacher's and she was the Deputy Head. The Head Teacher and older juniors were 'across the way' so over here she could be Headmistress of her very own little school. Naturally any misdemeanours over here were blamed upon me or my class as I was younger, greener and 'far less experienced'. I eventually learnt to grin and bear this, encouraged by nods and winks from knowing colleagues and assistants. Her first visit early on had rendered me entirely speechless. During one afternoon registration she marched into my class with two of my boys each welded to her vice-like hands.

"These boys," she began as the class hushed, "went OVER THE WALL. What are you going to do about that?"

Twenty five little pink faces swung towards me eager to hear what I was going to do about that. I was quite stupefied as my thoughts raced through the scaling of the Berlin Wall or escaping from Colditz Castle. I stared admiringly at the two heroic figures. I was quite impressed. 'What was this wall?' I wondered.

The Deputy Head continued, enraged by my silence.

"They may have been killed. That wall is at least two-and-a-half metres high and with a very hard landing on the road!"

I was even more impressed. They were only seven. She looked expectantly at me again and unable to think of anything remotely sensible to say I asked,

"Why did you go 'over the wall'?"

"It's the quickest way 'ome Miss," George patently muttered.

"We was late for lunch," added Gary in further explanation.

I hurriedly ad-libbed more admonishment, obeying the Deputy Head's unyielding stare.

"Well…It was a very dangerous thing to do. Jumping from that height on to a hard road might result in a broken ankle … or you might even land on a car … or be run over."

The hypnotising green eyes of the Deputy Head held mine a few moments more until she sensed surrender. She cleared her throat and turned to the boys.

"So. What are you going to do NEXT time you go home?"
The boys first looked puzzled but then George's eyes lit up.

"I know Miss, we'll climb over by the corner. There's a softer landing there!"

Home Sweet Home

To begin with I lived right in the heart of the village. I rented a room in a large cold Victorian house shared with other teachers and several field-mice. The tiny communal kitchen was the coldest room I'd ever been in, its only window facing a wall across a narrow passage way, which never saw the sun. The little field mice had a field day in there, routing through boxes of cereals abandoned by previous predators and scattering porridge oats across the cold stone tiles. Above the coldest kitchen ever was the coldest bathroom ever. A galvanised water tank hung precariously over the bath where icicles formed as the steam condensed on it.

I saw very little of the other teachers as they spent their evenings in the warmth of their friends' houses.

This newly qualified teacher moving into a quiet Cotswold village suddenly began to appreciate the free socialising taken for granted at college. The 'unwary' type might be in danger of throwing oneself into work and ending up a typical spinster schoolmistress. Being the 'wary' type I ventured out of my refrigerated container to scan the village notice-board. Distinctly unenthusiastic about the WI invitation for the longest weed, the Brownie Jumble Sale and the Ladies Brass Polishing, I opted for the Young Farmers meeting.

By the end of the evening I had been cajoled into joining their drama production, public speaking, stock-judging and quiz teams. Not satisfied with that the sports secretary Jo, kangaroo-bounced up to me after the meeting, announcing,

"You're playing hockey for us on Sunday. I'll pick you up – where do you live?"
I described my cold, mousey dwelling.

"Well you must come and stay with us at weekends – then you can't skive out of playing hockey. Besides you can't stay in that horrible house – it's full of teachers!"

Jo lived on a farm with several older siblings and other unusual animals. I first arrived on a dark Friday evening. Having negotiated a narrow path through an orchard (cleverly deduced after a hard meeting with an apple tree) I was confronted with a choice of two doors, both slightly ajar. 'Go straight in,' Jo had said. I took the leftmost and arrived in a cool whitewashed dairy. Two cats lapped delicately from a bowl of cream on the floor. On a table-top sat two wide enamel bowls of saffron-coloured milk, beside them a pair of butter pats, a jug of greyish buttermilk and three slabs of golden butter. The cats slunk out licking their whiskers and I was left in airy silence, contemplating which of the two latch-doors I should try next. Cautiously opening the larger door, I entered a scullery containing so many brooms, mops, basins, baler-twine balls, buckets, ironing boards, enamel jugs, saucepans, Burco boilers and twin-tubs that there was barely room to negotiate the narrow path between them and the sink.

As I passed the draining board I noticed at least 22 upturned mugs and wondered if Jo had hosted the whole hockey game.

Passing through another doorway – where the door had been removed from its hinges to form an 'open plan' effect – I found myself in an

enormous farm kitchen. In the near end was an enormous table which could amply seat the 22 mug users and opposite that a yellow Aga ticked happily away under steaming kettles. A small white enamel table stood between, with two overflowing mason basins cascading warm puffy white bread dough down the sides. The far end of the room was devoted to chairs, sofas, blankets and a TV talking away happily to itself. Halfway across the ceiling, suspended from a beam, was an old tractor-cab canvas presumably preventing the florescent light from reflecting onto the TV.

At first I thought the room was empty until I noticed a ginger cat, curled up in a ball and rising and falling like a ship on a swell. The sea was a woolly blue blanket. The blanket was pulled up around a corpse-like shape culminating in a large pair of black spectacles.

"Hiya," the spectacles said before turning back to watch the TV.

"Hi," I reciprocated.

I then noticed to my left, a pair of straw-specked red socks, also protruding from a blanket but at my eye-level and attached to a prone person in a precariously reclined garden-recliner.

"Oh hello dear!" squeaked a voice at my knees, "are you one of Jo's waifs and strays? I've made up some beds in the blue bedroom but don't move any of them around because there's a hole under the lino and you'll all end up in our front room – we don't want a mess!" the prone shape chuckled.

I didn't know quite how to respond to that immediately so she continued.

"Could you just tip my chair back upright for me, I get stuck sometimes. I've got to go out now and see to my pig. She's farrowing.

If I don't snip the piglets' tails off straight away they eat each other!" she laughed as the garden-recliner un-reclined itself to its upright pose.

The now visible person was a smiley middle-aged lady with curly blonde ringlets and a somewhat crooked nose, which I later learnt had been in a 'set to' with an angry bull. She pulled on some hand-knitted welly-warmers (made from 3 colours of wool), a straw-specked woolly hat, fingerless gloves, two coats and waterproof trousers before trundling out to the scullery.

"Hey, where's my wellies?" she squeaked.

A deeper voice answered from the depths of the scullery paraphernalia,

"They're where they always are Mother!"

"Oh yes."

The owner of the deep voice entered the kitchen followed by another, very silent, male. The one with the voice saw me and stared but before he spoke they both slid up onto the Aga top and sat warming themselves between the boiling kettles.

"Oo arr yoo then?" Speaking One asked in a Cotswold drawl.

"Jo invited me over," I answered a little defensively and feeling it necessitated further explanation continued, "I've just moved here – I teach at the village school."

"HA HA! A Little Miss!" Speaking One guffawed. "You gonna make us some tea then? Some of us 'av ter work for a living, not play with kiddywinks all day long!"

Ignoring the taunt I politely smiled back so he began making a pot of tea. Silent One sat motionless on the hot Aga presumably thawing out, hopefully in mind as well as body.

The two men had come indoors wearing their wellies, which were covered in a dirty grey dust. Indeed their whole bodies were covered in it including the lenses of Silent One's glasses. Perhaps he hadn't spoken because he couldn't actually see me.

Three mugs were snatched noisily off the draining board, and four tea bags preceded the water into a battered tin teapot with no lid.

"Cools quicker with no lid – in other words – can't find the lid!" and he laughed hilariously at his clever joke.

In the middle of this tea-making ceremony the scullery door burst open and a blue-uniformed nurse hurtled through the kitchen and rushed upstairs. Returning hurriedly downstairs, she grabbed a slab of fruitcake from a sideboard and rushed out again muttering,

"Can't stop – got a diabetic to jab!"

The two men completely ignored this interruption. Presumably it was commonplace.

As Speaking One poured the tea he scratched the grey dust out of his hair and it floated menacingly on top of each mugful.

"Don't worry" he laughed "it's only asbestos dust!"

I didn't drink my tea.

Welcome in the New

"Today we are welcoming a new boy," I announced to my class. Thirty curious heads spun round to stare at the poor newcomer who, having a very fair complexion, turned rapidly into a beetroot.

"His name is Laurie."

"Lorry?" muffled giggles muttered.

"My dad drives a lorry," Roy piped up proudly.

Bobby joined in.

"My dad's lorry is ginormous. E's took it to London today."

"He's 'taken' it," I corrected.

"No. 'e 'asn't stole it. It's HIS!" he worriedly replied.

"I've got a rabbit Miss," interjected Tobias proudly.

"I'm gonna be a lorry driver when I'm a man," drolled Roy.

"S..so'm I," Libby stammered.

"Ha! You'll never be a MAN – you'll be a MISSUS."

I intervened before complete madness ensued.

"Well Roy, perhaps you'd like to be Laurie's friend today and drive him around school until he knows his way."

Unfortunately for Laurie, Roy did exactly that for the entire day, pushing the new boy around the classroom, hands on his shoulders, executing grinding gears at every turn and accelerating his very noisy engine between tasks. Laurie didn't stay at the school for long.

An increasing number of commuting families were moving into the village especially from around London. These children were held in high esteem by the village girls mainly because they tended to wear different, shop-bought clothes rather than the usual home-mades or hand-me-downs. The lack of Cotswold droll in their voices also gave the children the impression that they were slightly superior.

"They must be really posh Miss, they says 'gararje' instead of 'garridge'!" They were considered highly desirable friends.

One such family arrived with immaculately turned-out flaxen-haired children, the youngest of whom, Sasha, joined my class, immediately becoming a magnet for girls and boys alike. Sasha quite innocently caused the biggest disaster of my teaching adventure.

Four boys in my class had fallen hopelessly in love with her and, of course, she completely ignored their strange advances causing them to invent new and exciting ways of attracting her attention. One of these was to slide snake-wise off their seats and under the table each time she passed. As it was beginning to become rather disruptive, I decided to intervene.

"Bobby, if you do that again, there won't be any football for you on Friday."
Several boys gasped in horror.
My statement was not altogether a falsehood. The Head had that morning informed me that the football match had been postponed and as I hadn't yet announced it to the class, felt I might use the news to my advantage for a while. Soon Bobby recklessly repeated his amorous advances slithering smoothly under the desk with a sideways glance at Sasha. An audible gasp rose up and 30 heads swung round to await my response – I had no choice.

"Bobby, EVERYONE heard me warn you. There will now be no football for you on Friday!"
Bobby's head slowly emerged from beneath the desk as the enormity of the disaster sank in, because despite being the youngest member of the school team he was the main goal scorer. He was vital for the team's success.

"Please Miss – " he pleaded as tears welled up and overcame him.
"He's GOT to play Miss."
"He's our best striker."
"No. He was told what would happen. He should have behaved himself, " I said turning away and innocently thinking the incident had closed. It hadn't.

And I hadn't expected the ferocity of the response from the parents. Next morning I was greeted with scowls and glares from a number of parents who normally didn't accompany their children to the school gate. Some refused to speak or even look at me whilst others muttered contemptuously.

"SHE don't know 'ow ter teach."
" No, 'tent fair what SHE did".
I tentatively approached the Head Teacher hoping for a bit of support, pleading,

"Surely this is all a fuss about nothing, the match is cancelled anyway."
"Ah …" the Head faltered stroking his chin. "Actually the match is now back on again, I forgot to tell you. You … er … couldn't change your mind and let him play?"
"Well, no. I'd lose complete control if I back-tracked now."
"Well yes, I suppose. It's entirely your decision, I'll leave it in your hands," he said, not exactly brimming with confidence.
Back outside, Bobby's mum stormed over.

"Football's the only thing 'e comes ter school for, 'e should be encouraged, not put down like that!"

And she stomped away with a group of mumbling followers, none I think, ever speaking to me again, even to this day. As I turned to go back inside I felt a little tug on my sleeve and a little slip of a lady whispered,

"I think you're right. It's an honour to play for your school and should be earned by good behaviour as well as good play." She was my only supporting voice but unfortunately as everyone had now left, no-one else heard her.

The match was lost. Also lost was a substantial amount of respect and support from an influential group of parents. I had completely under-estimated the importance of football in such a rural setting. It was so sacred that a few years later when our two footballing teachers were replaced by two outstanding (but non-sporty) teachers, a group of parents staged a protest at their appointment.

Sasha continued to be completely oblivious of her involvement in the whole affair and eventually fell in love with a potter.

Funetix and Eemerjunt Ryting

Parents often grumbled about our mysterious 'modern methods' and particularly the way we taught writing. (Some of the parents had been taught with a slate and chalk.)

Our aim was to get the children to express themselves on paper as early and naturally as possible. The method we used is called 'Emergent Writing' and as most parents misunderstood it I will belatedly describe how it develops.

A child's first attempts at writing look like this _ _ _ _ and they gradually develop vague letter shapes, characteristically O I O O I, at about school starting age or before. Building on this the teacher will say, 'Tell me what you have written under your picture' and write the correct version under the child's – not correcting it (the first parent grizzle).

This may go on for several weeks but eventually recognisable words 'emerge' as the child's reading skills develop in earnest. Help is given when they ask for words and they are given their own wordbooks to refer to – but still no 'corrections' as such are made.

By about junior level, simple mis-spelt words are corrected but allowing the writing to 'flow' before correction (major parent gripe as they think this is just 'learning to spell wrong').

Our corrected scripts were then copied in neat handwriting onto best paper, sometimes in ink, and with a carefully measured 1cm border, decorated with an appropriate handwriting pattern. This 'best work' was displayed on the wall or in their class-made folders.

Naturally, it was never this beautifully presented work that the parents homed in on but the mis-spelt rough version in their workbooks. One Open Evening Sasha's mum (the new family from London) pulled me up on the spelling in Sasha's rough book.

"Why can't you teach them to spell, Sasha's put 'wow' instead of 'well'?"

"That's because to keep the flow of their writing we teach them initially to spell phonetically – as it sounds – and 'well' sounds like 'wow' with her accent," I explained

"Aksint?" she squawked, hand on hip, "we aint got no aksint. We're fwom Landin!"

Grammar Rules OK

"As the ages and abilities of my class spanned several years, when formal instruction was required it was easiest to select little groups showing 'readiness'. The children enjoyed these short cosy sessions around a small easel in the carpeted and cushioned Home Corner. As practising teachers will know though, formal lesson-plans never go quite as the lesson-plan plans them to.

Silent e Lesson 1

  "These letters are all 'vowels'." I instructed, writing on the board, "Let's first say their sounds, a e i o u and their names ay ee eye oh yoo."
 The children chanted obediently.
  "Now we're going to pretend these vowels are children and the other letters, 'consonants' are grown-ups."
The children smiled back at their fellow vowels and frowned at the grown-up consonants.
  "Put together, they can make words, like the t-a-p in this story."
The children shuffled bottoms until they were sitting comfortably.
  "T, a and p were riding on a bus ," I began,
  "I hate buses. I like riding on my dad's lorry," moaned Roy.
  I continued.
  "At the bus-stop 'e' got on. He's called 'silent e',"
  "Why Miss?"
  "Because this 'e' doesn't speak and neither should you."

"Like Shaun Miss – he doesn't speak?"

"Yes, like Shaun. Anyway 'silent e' got on the bus and sat in front of 'p'," I said writing t-a-p-e, "and 'silent e' being a very naughty vowel, stretched his long arm right over 'p' and pinched 'a'," I said, drawing an appropriate arm.

"This makes 'a' shout his name out …"

"Ay!" they chorused.

"…and so 'tap' turns into 'tape'" I said, with satisfaction at the delivered lesson. We tried other words …

'den' into 'dene'

"Eee!" they chorused.

'sit' into 'site'

"Eye!"

'cop' into cope

"Oh!"

'cut' into 'cute'

"Yooo!"

"Great!" I applauded, "You've got it! Lesson complete."

"Miss? – what if 'e' wanted to sit at the back of the bus and wave at the cars?" asked Roy.

"Yeah. It wouldn't say 'site' then, it'd say 'esit' Max smugly argued.

"There's an EXIT at the back anyway, a mergissy exit where you escape when it crashes!" Roy exclaimed. Hoping to stop my whole lesson crashing I intervened,

"He wouldn't sit at the back anyway."

"Why Miss?"

"Because he gets travel sick." I quickly improvised.

"Ahh!" the girls sympathised.

Edward, turning a little pale added,

"I was travel sick on the bus once, all over the seat."

The group suddenly grew subdued and began to turn a little green, at which point we proceeded out to play.

Silent e Lesson 2

(Lesson notes – don't mention travel sickness again.)

"Sometimes," I began, " 'silent e' is so naughty that the grown-ups have to get in his way to stop him pinching the other vowels." Interest was high – the children loved naughtiness.

"F, a and t were riding on the bus. 'Silent e' sat in front of 't' then reached over and pinched 'a',"

"Ay!" the children chorused, "now it says 'fate'."

"but then," I continued, Mr r and his friend Mr t got on the bus. Mr t sat next to Mrs t so 'silent e' 's long arm couldn't reach 'a' any more and 'a' stopped shouting its name again." I animated the story on the board.

"Fatter!" they squealed but Max looked puzzled.

"What if Mr t didn't want to sit by Mrs t and Mr r sat there instead – it wouldn't spell the word properly then?"

"Neh – cos my dad wouldn't sit next to my mum on the bus, she's too fat!" Roy snorted.

"And my mum won't sit with my dad cos she likes a gossip with her friends," giggled Jane.

"My mum likes a gossip with the postman. I gets sent out ter play when he comes," added Tony grumpily and at this point I decided we should all go out to play.

Introducing the Apostrophe. Lesson 1

With a smaller select group of 'readies' I drew a large apostrophe on our little easel.

"Do you know what this is called?" I asked.

"A tadpole Miss."

"My dad calls 'em Pollyblobs."

"No they're Pollybobbles!"

I re-aligned proceedings by showing them some in a book.

"It's called an a p o s t r o p h e," I slowly enunciated.

"A Posh Trophy," they slowly chorused.

"Pollyblob ... " a single inattentive voice echoed then blushed profusely. I battled on unabashed.

"We'll call this one the Naughty Apostrophe," I suggested re-drawing the big wiggle and placing two goggly eyes on top – a rash mistake forever regretted as goggle-eyed apostrophes adorned their written-work for months afterwards.

"In your writing, when someone is speaking, you can shorten what they are saying by pushing some of their letters out of their words. That's what the Naughty Apostrophe does." Blank faces stared back so I illustrated on the little easel.

"'Tom is running' is shortened to 'Tom's running' when the Naughty Apostrophe pushes 'i' out of the dinner queue."

"Ugh!" gasped the girls, "that's really naughty!"

The boys looked puzzled.

"Was Tom running to get to the front of the dinner queue?"

"Probably," I answered uncertainly.

"Did he get there before the Posh Trophy?" Gary asked.

"Yes," I answered, unsure quite where this was going.

"But Tom would get sent to the back anyway if he was running," Tony frowned.

"And if Posh Trophy was hungry, why didn't he push in at the front?" asked Bobby worriedly.

"Didn't want teacher to see 'im praps," Tony suggested.

"Yeah! Else," Gary added.

"Is it dinner time yet Miss?" sighed Tony.

The Apostrophe (Possessive) Lesson 2

(Lesson Notes (1) Best not to mention dinner.

(2) Do *not* draw eyes on the apostrophe)

"The apostrophe is also used when something BELONGS to someone," I related to an even smaller 'ready' group, "like 'John's puppy'," I wrote, to John's satisfied grin.

"This time the Naughty Apostrophe has pushed two people out of the di… the queue, 'h' and 'i' because it should say 'John his puppy'."

"That's not right Miss because if it were Jane's it would say 'Jane her puppy' and there's no 's' in that," Sasha cleverly deduced. As I paused to think of a 'hers' explanation the children continued.

"No it is right. Cos it weren't Jane's puppy. It were John's. He got given it to cheer him up because he had the Chicken Pox."

"Well he should've been given a chicken then, shouldn't he?" Max concluded.

Our Last Apostrophe Lesson

"The Naughty Apostrophe DOES push in at the front of the queue this time," I began, to the immense satisfaction of the boys.

"If something belongs to more than one person we write it like this … 'boys' shorts' because they belong to more than one boy."

"Do they share them then Miss?" Gary asked.

"They must be poor if they have to share shorts," Sasha frowned sadly.

"My mum says it's not very nice to share shorts – it's not hygienical," sneered Jane screwing up her nose.

"You CAN share football shorts," Bobby snarled in her face "our kit gets washed all togever an you just grabs any pair out the bag!"

"Miss! Miss!" Tony bounced, shooting his hand up in the air, "Miss – me mum washed all me dad's teams' red and white kit altogever an' the shorts all came out pink!" and he rolled around on the carpet spluttering hysterically for several stitch-making seconds before he could deliver his punch line "… an they STILL 'ad ter play in them!"

Dressed for Christmas

Village schools in the '70s rarely had a proper uniform although there were always a few children sent in the synonymous grey shorts and jumper or the standard pinafore more familiar to their mothers' schooldays.

Mostly they wore knitwear lovingly crafted by nimble-fingered aunts or grandmothers. Cable-stitched bobbly Arans and elaborate lace-knits ranged down to thrifty stocking-stitched odd-balls with multi-coloured stripes or contrasting sleeves where the colour ran out. A metre of remnant cotton print from the market would make two elastic-waist skirts or a straight shift dress and Mum's voluptuous outdated Laura Ashley maxi-dress would fabricate fully-flared skirts and puff-sleeved blouses, as well as cushion covers and table mats.

Less needle-wise mums frequented the village jumble sales. Rupert wore a dainty powder blue pearl-buttoned sweater for a whole year until Rosie told him it used to be hers.

It seemed that the more 'well to do' the families were, the more cheaply they were apt to dress their children. These families were especially averse to buying sportswear, stuffing old play-clothes into their children's PE bags. Even the drawstring bags were made out of old curtains!

Only a very few (in that era termed the 'upwardly mobile') families presented their children in immaculate quality clothing for school despite them constantly returning home paint-splattered. (One of these such children is now a buyer for a top national clothes chain.)

This lack of uniform and casual approach to dress meant that on more special public occasions we needed to smarten the children up a bit. Our annual Carol Service was staged in the village church and with solo items, recorder pieces, readings and class choirs singing it was quite a formal occasion. The church flower ladies made a worthy effort with holly and ivy, a stepped stage was carpentered by a 'chippy' dad and special lighting set up by a 'sparky' dad, as it was an evening service requiring 'spots' – he said.

As the occasion approached the school day was filled with soloists singing, readers reading, pipers piping, choirs carolling and producers panicking.

On the day of the concert we gathered the children together in assembly and the Head announced,

"We would like you all to wear your very best clothes for the Carol Service as it is a very special occasion and you all deserve too, to look and feel special." Wiping a sentimental tear from his eye he continued, "So please wear your very best clothes – best shirts, best dresses, best jumpers," he enthused.

Billy the soloist's hand shot up.

"I 'ent got no best clothes Sir!"

"Well … er … wear your favourite clothes then."

On the cold, crisp night of the concert the church glowed warm and welcoming, strung with holly and ivy and cascades of red ribbon. Shiny scrubbed children arrived and found their places on the spot-lit stage wearing an array of itchy Fair-Isles, crimson party dresses with matching ribbons, tight waistcoats and choking ties. Paul looked just like robin redbreast perched up there in his scarlet jumper and brown corduroys.

Last to enter were the two main soloists who would stand centre stage right under the spotlights.

Derek and Billy marched proudly down the church aisle. They were dressed in the complete Wolverhampton Wanderers' kit – bright yellow shirts, black shorts, waspy black and yellow striped socks and matching football boots.

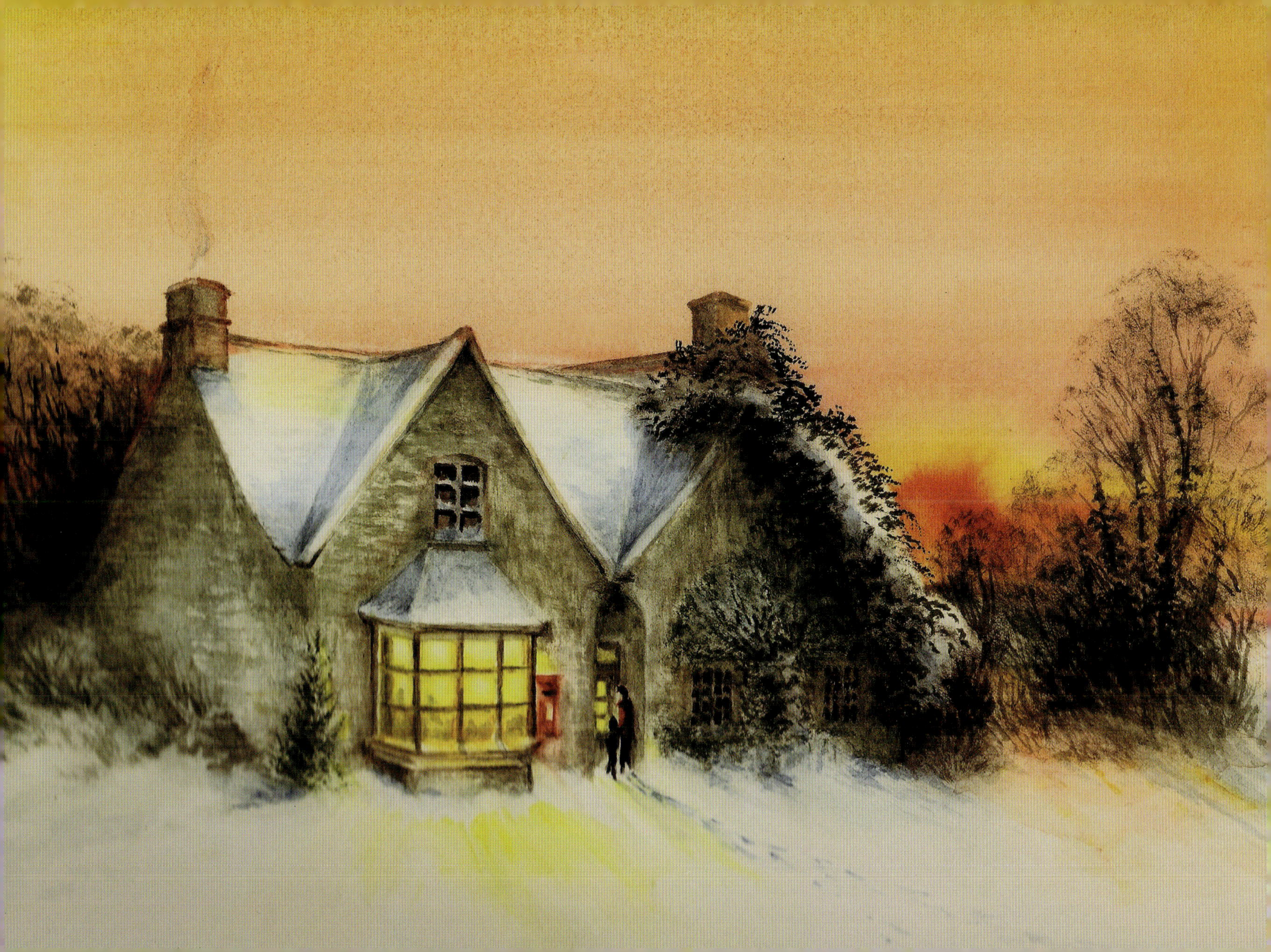

Spring Term

I'm in Charge

The smooth day-to-day operation of a primary school rests in the hands of a supremely gifted and multi-talented leader. But it's not the Head. As all teachers know, it's the caretaker. Who else could always fix the boiler, find keys, mend windows, un-block blocked toilets, mend water leaks, restore whiteness to powder-paint-pink sinks, fetch footballs off the roof, catch mice, catch the cat and generally keep unwanted wildlife (including teenagers) off the premises?

I'm in Charge 33

On top of all of this – they polish wooden floors to Olympic ice-rink standard, polish brass inkwells so children can pull faces in them and disinfect the whole school to hospital standard (or perhaps better).

With our caretaker, these duties and more were happily and willingly done when volunteered but if you absentmindedly asked her, however kindly, a strange dark demon emerged and engulfed the happy persona.

During an after-school staff meeting – during the essential tea and cakes pre-meeting to be more precise – a long queue of bubbling children began a sustained crescendo outside the frosted window. Mrs Broome, our broom-laden caretaker popped her head around the door.

"Lollipop Lady 'ent 'ere yet," she stated, swish-swashing her broom.

"She still ent 'ere," she added two biscuits later.

Now, what the Head *should* have done was to pause and wait for her 'shall I do it?' but in a moment of madness he asked with a cake-filled mouth,

"Could *you* do it – we're all a bit busy just now?"

Mrs Broome rested both her hands on her broom-handle and glared solemnly back.

"Well," she began as the demon metamorphosed, "before coming to a decision regarding that request I shall have to communicate with my Union Representative at Union Headquarters. If I may be allowed some privacy I will use your telephone for an Official Call." So we dutifully filed out of the room and chattered amongst ourselves in the cold entrance hall whilst the children's teeth chattered in the cold outside.

Ten minutes elapsed during which three children were ushered inside – one for throwing a snowball at the window, another for squashing a snowball down Rosie's neck and the third with hands so cold they resembled aubergines.

Mrs Broome was heard to put the phone down but then stood in the doorway preventing our return. She took a deep breath …

"The Official Position regarding the ongoing situation is this … ," she began as the queue of cold children rioted outside,

"My Union Representative instructs me that Under the Terms of my Employment I am not required to do Lollipop Lady duties. In addition, if the Lollipop Lady is on an Official Strike I will have to come out in sympathy with her – AND I'LL NOT CROSS PICKET LINES!" she frowned, "However," she quietened, " I have rung the said Lollipop

Lady and she is rather indisposed with her 'troubles' so I am now awaiting an Official Reply from my union before I make any pronouncements." The phone rang and she shut the door again.

"It seems," she said emerging, "that At This Moment in Time I represent the only one here with suitable qualifications to hold the lollipop BUT THEY INSIST that if I carry out these extra duties I must wear the Full Safety Uniform – for insurance purposes – to include Fluorescent Hat, Gloves and Jacket!" and she marched off to the uniform cupboard rattling her Very Important Bunch of Keys.

Our usual lollipop lady was quite a robust, substantially-built person so when the diminutive Mrs Broome emerged fully attired all you could see was her little round nose and pert mouth. Her hands were hidden somewhere up the voluptuous sleeves so she had to grip the lollipop in a vice between two arms and her feet slid along the floor under the bell-tent coat.

"Come along Children. From this moment in time I am your Union Recognised Official Crossing Patrol Warden until the normal situation resumes to normal circumstances … again."

She proudly glided to the middle of the snowy, empty, road and raised her lollipop aloft.

Twenty children marched briskly across the still empty road and ran home cheering. Mrs Broome's moment of glory had ended.

The Scourge of the Ice-breaker

There was another duty that Mrs Broome undertook with extreme dedication. She saw it as her sole responsibility to prevent anyone slipping on school ice. She hated ice with a vengeance.

Towards the beginning of winter she had begun to collect and secrete her weapons – buckets, brooms, salt, waterproof gloves, woolly socks and wellies were hoarded and locked away in a bulging wooden shed awaiting the onslaught of the ice crystals. Her only safe and secret spy was the BBC Weatherman – the only trusted ally who could anticipate the attack – and she WOULD be ready for the battle.

Our large playground had a gentle slope down from the field and at its top corner the field would slowly trickle its moisture in a steady flow across the grey tarmac to the shed. In cold spells it froze and formed the most glorious slide imaginable with the wooden shed as a safety buffer at the end. This was now her battleground. She had to arrive first with her salt before the children could polish it to glassy perfection with expertly executed *glissandos*. The children soon calculated that her arrival in the morning could be substantially delayed by tactical bribery of her son to feign forgetting his books, or even illness, to force a return home. Mrs Broome cleverly counteracted this by salting the playground the evening before, acting upon information supplied by her special agent in the BBC.

This move was rebuffed by boys with buckets of water leading to the happy discovery that black ice was not only less detectable but made a far more deadly slide.

"Emergency Action is now required before any fatalities occur!" Mrs Broome announced to the Head.

"I must re-arm with a better weapon. I need Gritter Lorry Grit. Gritter Lorry Grit will defeat them. The situation is now urgent. CHILDREN MIGHT DIE!"

The following day an expensive concrete bunker was built at the top of the playground and the boys read the dreaded word GRIT imprinted on its side. They stood solemnly watching as an expensive load of Gritter Lorry Grit arrived in Roy's dad's dumper truck. No amount of water buckets could wash that away. Mrs Broom sighed in happy victory.

The expensive Gritter Lorry Grit was however, never used. Winter played itself out with a mild and wet spell so instead the boys made a massive mud-slide on the sloping field. As the field was Parish Council property Mrs Broome held no responsibility for it and so took no interest whatsoever in the children's safety thereon.

Smile Please

"Tomorrow it will be School Photograph time."
That year the decision had been made to allow the children to be photographed with brothers, sisters or cousins to make a 'family' photograph if they wished (it would save on both money and wall-space). It emerged however, that Tamsin would be the only child posing on her own and she wasn't at all happy about it.

"Snot fair!" she whimpered. "Shan't come to school."

"Please *do* come. It'll be a proper 'portrait' with just you in the picture – rather special," I encouraged. She was unimpressed. So was her mother who cunningly approached the Head blinking her long eyelashes and imploring,

"Tamsin has such a sensitive nature and has real 'issues' about being an 'only child'. May she be photographed with our dog?"
Tamsin's mother had studied Child Psychology. She continued pleading with the Head in an enticing whisper.

"We can creep in secretly before school, then afterwards I can slip quickly away with the dog – and no-one need know."
Tamsin's mother evidently knew a little about adult psychology too as the Head melted like butter.

The canine getaway was delayed somewhat though as Tamsin's dog turned out to be an enormous slobbering Newfoundland, necessitating a re-arrangement of the 'set' to accommodate Tamsin in the portrait. Juxtaposed to the dog's silken ears, Tamsin's newly combed hair then began to rise up in a static pyramid requiring a rapid watering down. This further delayed proceedings by demanding a meticulous removal of hair, water droplets and dog slobber from the dark drapes.

Finally, job done, Tamsin's mother and hound slipped swiftly out of the back door to the public footpath, quite unnoticed.

The poor photographer, clearly ruffled by his adventure into pet portraiture had to be revived with black coffee (and three sugars) by which time the rest of the school had arrived outside. As expected due to the extra sibling accompaniments there was somewhat increased playground babble so the Head went out to restore a little order.

Astonished, he was greeted by a chaotic menagerie of fur, feather and child. Interwoven dogs chased retaliating cats; children clutched terrified tortoises; a parrot in a cage squeaked obscenities at a chicken and a blow-dried pet lamb in a pink harness bleated mistakenly at a poodle.

"Clearly news travels fast in the animal kingdom," said the Head after a few speechless seconds, "What on earth have we got here?"

"I've got a rabbit," said Tobias.

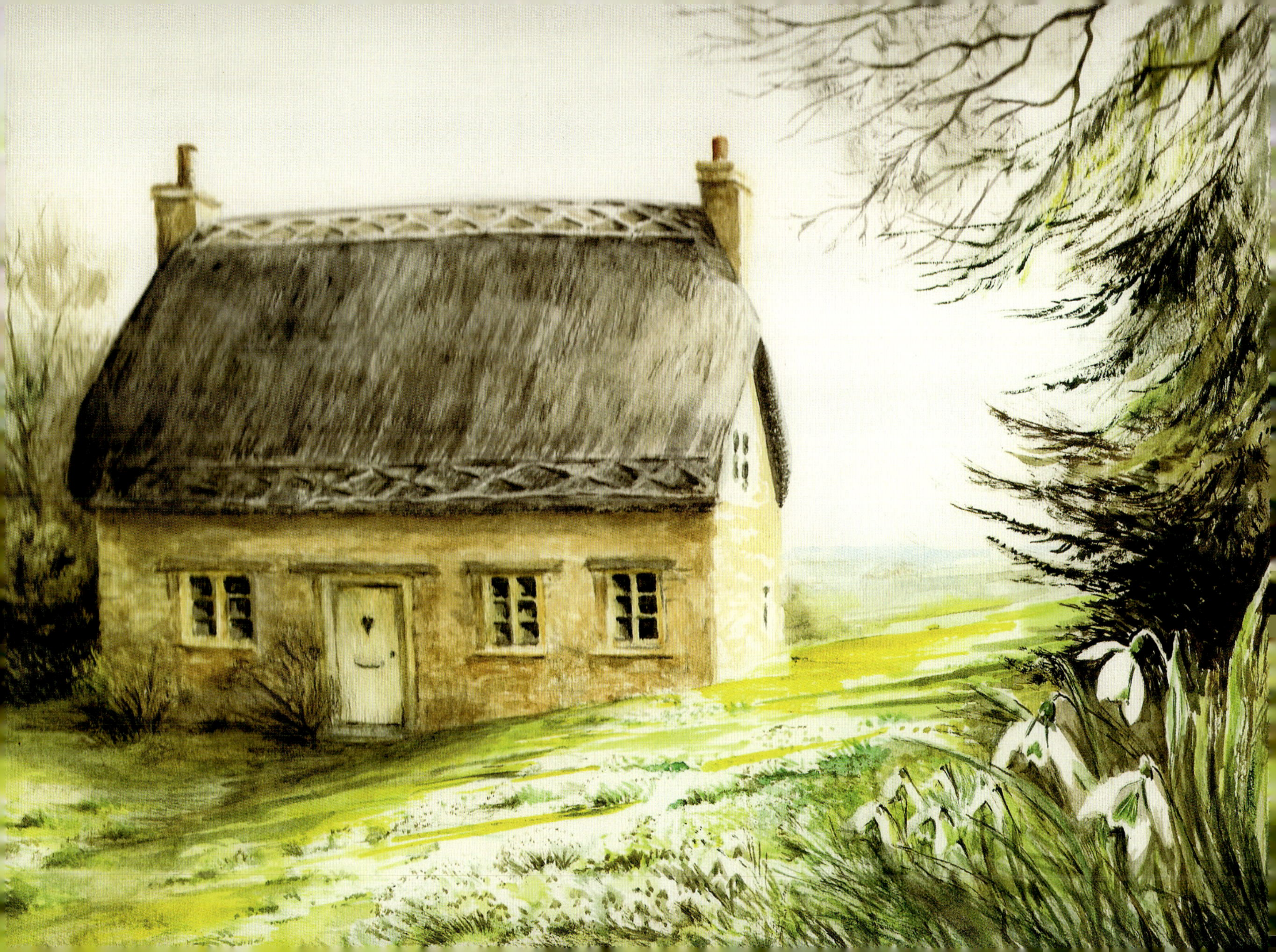

A Mad Menagerie

Do strange pets reflect strange owners – or is it vice-versa I wonder?

It was after several visits to Jo's farm before I first met Tip – precisely at five minutes past four on a Sunday afternoon - just as Jo's flapjacks were emerging from the Aga and just before many greedy mouths were burned. I heard the scullery door open and an icy draft brought in a very waggy, grinning sheepdog.

"Shut that door, Tip," Jo ordered and back he trotted and shut the door, retiring to the sofa only to be followed by another icy blast.

"Tip, shut it PROPERLY."

He dutifully shut the door with a sharp 'click' this time and headed back to the sofa landing unnoticed on the prone Speaking One in his customary sleeping state. After a few deftly performed wriggles Tip settled himself between the sofa back and Speaking One's back, slowly wriggling a space until he lay in it, wedged upside down and grinning cheekily backwards towards me.

"He's not finished yet – wait and see," Jo chuckled.

After a few minutes passed, to ensure Speaking One was soundly asleep again, Tip turned and began paddling his paws gently into the sleeping body until it slipped, still sleeping, onto the floor mat. The Victorious Tip stretched out across the whole sofa whilst the oblivious Speaking One slept soundly on the floor.

"Oh Tip's back," said Annie entering with full pig-farrowing attire.

"Has he been lost then, I haven't ever seen him before?" I asked.

"No, he spends weekends away with his mistress," she replied as if in complete explanation and reclined to sleep. Jo had to continue.

"Every Friday afternoon – at precisely five minutes to four he trots across the fields to a weekenders' cottage and meets them just as they arrive with their Labrador, Jade. They're totally in love and inseparable all weekend – he even shares her food. The family leaves at four o'clock and he trots home again. After that he's no good for anything until at least Tuesday – dirty stop out!" Jo said munching a flapjack.

At least three cats lived at the farm too. In addition to the sea-faring ginger cat there were two beautiful blue tabbies, a mother and kitten.

One day the house-loving mother uncharacteristically went missing leaving a noisy, pining youngster. To deliver rapid relief from this caterwauling we were all engaged in a search. Cupboards and corners, sheds and barns, garden and orchard all revealed nothing.

"She's never stayed away this long before – something must have happened," sniffed Annie but recovering quickly she set to making the bread. She lifted off the lid of the huge enamel flour tin and squealed with delight as a flour-dusted blue cat's head appeared with a rather disgruntled look in its sharp green eyes.

The morning after the mother cat's return the traumatised kitten was discovered missing and now the distraught mother caterwauled noisily up and down the kitchen.

Annie had been out all night with a pig – a new gilt with her first litter – and as the cat was preventing her 'catch-up' sleep she decided instead to continue her bread-making.

"Can you reach down and get my dough out of the bottom of the Aga – it should be risen, it's been there all night."

I opened the bottom Aga door and retrieved a large mason basin. There in the middle of the cushioning warm dough was the little blue kitten, fast asleep and happily snoring contentedly.

"Oh what a perfect little nest!" exclaimed Annie and then proceeded to make bread rolls out of the furry blue dough.

Something Scary in the Scullery

Cats, dogs and humans were not the only animals I have met in Jo's kitchen. I'd taken some marking with me to the farm hoping to squeeze some work in, between Jo's sports fixtures. Whilst I sat ticking at the table Annie was snoozing before her next pig call-up and Speaking One was, as usual, asleep on the sofa.

My sense of alarm was alerted suddenly by a soft padding noise in the scullery then a slow soft breathing. Recent news of a Big Cat in the area pricked at my thoughts and I sat motionless waiting for the pounce. Neither sleeper stirred as I watched the door-less doorway.

To my horror a large black head peered around the corner and blinked two curly eye-lashes as it licked its grey nose with a fat pink tongue. Slightly perturbed I crept slowly over to the sofa and nudged Speaking One.

"Hey. Wake up. There's a cow in the scullery."
One eye slowly opened and met two eyes in the doorway. A brief moment elapsed whilst thoughts were gathered.

"Mother! Mother, wake up. There's a cow in the scullery," Speaking One reported matter-of-factly.

"Yes dear."

"Mother there's a COW in the SCULLERY," he repeated slowly.

"A what? A cow!" a flummoxed Annie spluttered, tipping herself upright.

" Hey, there's a cow in the scullery! Get out now!" she squealed waving her arms about but the pretty Jersey cow just blinked, slowly licking each nostril in turn.

"Where's Jason?" Annie flapped and ran to the hall, "Jason?" she called up the stairs "... it's four o'clock!"
Annie returned to her recliner and reclined.

"It's alright," she said to me, "she's just come in to tell us it's milking time, I expect she wants her tea."

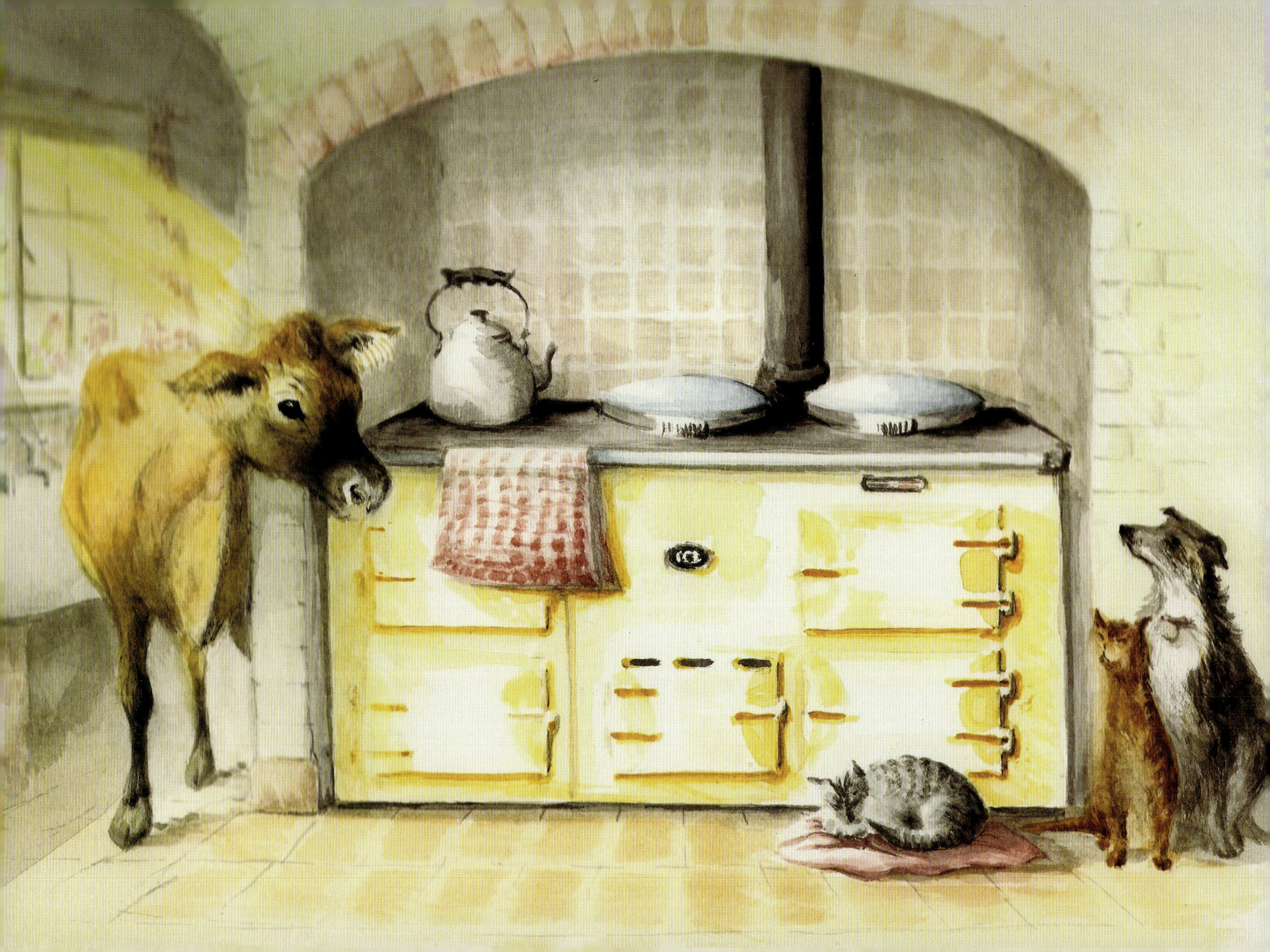

On the Topic of Time

As I mentioned before, our school had no uniform. If it had, I would not have been able to identify the culprit.

We were doing an extended topic about Time – clock time, growth, measuring and life-cycles and to start it off I had set up a large display on shelves and tables. It began as a 'hands on' experience but my own lack of experience resulted in a resort to a 'look only' experience, mainly to prolong the lives of the captive tadpoles and caterpillars. I had also placed various types of clocks and other timepieces on a shelf above the tables – candle clocks, sundials and my own alarm clock with its two shiny brass bells. It was fully wound but with the alarm silenced with the catch 'on'. This made it quite irresistible to the experimenting children but as you have probably gathered, I was still quite 'green'.

Timmy always wore a custard yellow jumper to school, knitted by his gran. It was a very useful colour because I could always see it out of the corner of my eye when it was wandering in places it shouldn't have been wandering in.

I was listening to Callum reading when the custard yellow jumper sidled up to the tadpole tank. Seconds later a quick flash of yellow shot into a chair. This was quickly followed by a shrill alarm bell and a momentous splash, then green water splattering across the room. The clanging bells transformed their sound into a bubbly gargle as my shiny blue alarm clock sank slowly to the bottom of the tadpole tank with large bubbles surfacing from its face and curious tadpoles engaging in conversation with the black numbers. Timmy sat in horror. With his bright yellow jumper and glowing red face, he looked just like a bowl of rhubarb and custard.

There's None so Queer as Folk

Returning to Jo's after a squash match, we followed a smoky campervan as it trundled up the drive. As it stopped, out jumped six children of varying heights wearing multi-coloured jumpers, shorts and sandals. A grey-haired bespectacled driver, also in shorts and sandals, then helped a grandmotherly figure down from the high front seat, handing her a large woven bag. Jo smiled politely and we followed them into the kitchen.

"G'day Annie – got some spring water for me?" an Australian drone asked.

"Yes dear, help yourself," Annie squeaked from her reclined recliner and the man disappeared whilst the old lady switched on the TV, sat down and extracted knitting needles and a rainbow tangle of wool balls from her woven bag. Without saying a word she proceeded to knit, click clicking away while Annie went back to sleep.

A little while later the bespectacled Australian arrived back and glanced out into the vegetable garden where six rose-faced children were running wildly out of control.

"Got any nice veggies out there Annie?"

"Yes dear. Grab a box from the scullery and help yourselves."

He returned again overflowing with cabbages, carrots and sprouts.

"I saw some eggs in the scullery – right next to the butter so I helped myself – that alright Annie? Thanks a lot m'dear, see you soon."

At this cue the old lady rolled up her knitting, threw the wool in her bag, switched off the TV and left without a word. Outside the six runaway children were rounded up and the campervan smoked noisily away.

Annie chuckled from her recliner.

"Are they relatives?" I asked Annie.

"No. They just turned up one day asking for some spring water for their little boy who's got eczema. They've been coming here regular as clockwork ever since. Haven't got a clue who they are!"

We Are ALL Special

Several children in the school had 'special needs' with problems more severe than in most mainstream schools. This was due to the sympathetic attitude of our Head. The whole school was taught that each of these children was 'special' in a good way and their individual needs and privileges were explained carefully to each class. Occasionally, other children could become temporarily 'special' if they had accidents or became ill and they too would receive special privileges and bonuses.

After informing my class of a newly arrived special child Tony piped up.

"Miss I'm speshoo."

"Are you Tony?"

"Yeah ... I 'ad me mouth sewn up when I was a babby. That's why I can't speak proper!" he proudly announced curling up his top lip with a grubby hand to reveal a scar from a neatly repaired cleft lip.

"Speshoo people go to the FRONT of dinner queue," he said expectantly.

"Alright then Tony – you can be first in the class dinner queue in future," I agreed and he beamed with satisfaction.

Tony was a stocky lad with big strong limbs, a large brow and a long nose, unbefitting for a small boy but which would eventually evolve into a very handsome young man. For now though, the girls hated him and he hated them. He said, in fact, that he hated everything. "I 'ates school," he grumbled every day upon arrival but now at the front of our dinner queue he was smiling glibly at the girls behind him as he marched in front for lunch. This continued for the rest of the week but I noticed the girls taking a pace or two back on his blustery arrival and turning away from him. He began to look a lonely figure up there at the front. At the beginning of the following week he sidled up to me and folded his tree-trunk arms grumpily. A big tear rolled down his large plump cheekbone and sad eyes looked pleadingly at me.

"What's the matter Tony?"

"I 'ates being at the front Miss. I do' wanna be speshoo anymore," he sobbed.

"Oh? Why not Tony?"

"There's all girls at the front an' they won't play. I wanna go to the back of the queue so's I can push everyone an' be naugh'y. I likes being naugh'y Miss."

"I'll see what I can do about it Tony."

Lunch time arrived and the hustle of tidy up began. I said in my loudest stern voice,

"Tony. You are a very naughty boy. You must go to the back of the dinner queue from now on!"

He was delighted.

"Ugh Miss – " he groaned "I 'ates schoow."

Tony continued to hate school until an ex-teacher parent offered to take my girls for games lessons leaving me with the boys. With smaller numbers we could do some real football skills.

"Ugh. You can't teach football Miss," groaned Tony and grumbled away all through the skills practice at how useless I was.

"We'll finish with a short game!" I announced in exasperation as another ball disappeared over the hedge.

"You can pick one team Tony and show me how good a captain you can be. I'm sure you can do it far better than I."

Something then completely transformed Tony. The other captain just picked his friends but Tony's eyes scrutinised the squad and carefully selected his team – the tallest boy for goalkeeper, tall stocky defenders, two fast wingers and two small sprinters as strikers. He placed himself midfield and straightaway took charge of the game. The slow, reluctant cumbersome body became an animated coach, encouraging, instructing, pointing and refereeing, leaving me a useless onlooker. He had absolute respect from all the boys.

"Great game Tony!" they applauded and embraced each other with a manly, footbally hug.

"I likes football Miss…but I still 'ates schoow," Tony grinned.

I wonder which football team he's coaching now.

A Bit of Helpful Advice

From time to time, usually a very inconvenient time, School Advisers would arrive to give the school advice on things they felt we should be advised on – like families, health, or on subjects like art, PE or handwriting.

To get my full cooperation I had been forewarned of a visit from an advisor who was to take a handwriting lesson, so I too forewarned the children in the hope of getting their full cooperation.

"Mr Palmer's coming to do some hand writing," I announced clearly. Timmy may have misheard because he began giggling uncontrollably. I ignored him, fearing further explanation might worsen his decorum even more.

We sharpened pencils, wiped the tables clean and found nice, uncreased white pages in their workbooks as The Advisor was known to be a little fussy.

The adviser swooped in, in his usual flamboyant manner and dramatically wrote a sentence on the board in beautiful Italic writing.

"RIGHT children! Sit up STRAIGHT, feet FLAT, books FLAT, pages STRAIGHT and PENCILS pointing over your SHOULDER. Copy THAT!" he said dancing around the tables examining pencils.

"Too sharp!"

"Too short!"

"Too blunt!"

"Too black!"

His 'bounciness' was beginning to annoy some of the more down-to-earth boys and despite my raised-eyebrow-warning they began to play up. Roy snapped his pencil tip noisily and Gary catapulted his pencil across the room sending it cart-wheeling over Mr. Palmer's head.

"Who did that?" the ruffled advisor spurted, spinning round in a rather feminine flap.

"Roy!" accused Gary.

"Gary!" accused Roy.

"Please call me by my name when you answer," Mr Palmer's now nervous, quavering voice admonished.

"Your name is Mr. Pyjamas!" Timmy squealed curling up in a heap of giggles and consequently infecting the whole class. The lesson ended in hilarious uproar.

'Mr. Pyjamas' did not visit us again.

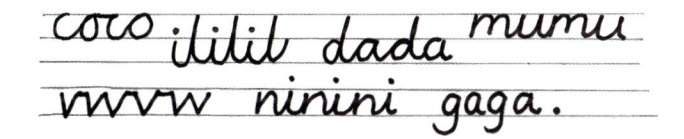

coco ililil dada mumu vwvw ninini gaga.

Many of the county health or social advisors came from the council offices far away in the city and seemed to be rather nervous about coming 'out to the sticks'. They had strange preconceptions about our rural life. Farming families in particular bothered them, as they didn't really understand their attitude towards animals as a business. They also considered their practical farmhouses far too ramshackle and unkempt. One tried to talk enthusiastically about farming to Jake and spoke of her visit to a farm museum with its beautiful yellow-painted wagon, milk-maids on stools and downy ducklings. Jake's father ran the local estate's 1000 sow pig-unit.

"Do all your piglets have names?" she asked him.

Drawing a blank she turned to me, "There's a new little boy joining your school soon and I'd like you to keep a little eye open on him," she said. "He's from a farm you know," she added in hushed tones.

Another time I had a visit from a social worker attached to family whose children were in my class. The children (Gary and his sister) were busy and hard working if a little mischievous. My only educational concern was that they needed more reading support at home and much less TV whilst inactively ensconced on their old sofa.

"Even just a few minutes reading with Mum or Dad on the old sofa would reap dividends," I suggested.

Their house was definitely scruffy and the children often dirty but both parents worked hard even if Dad's job 'out in 'is van' was a little dubious. I felt sure that with a little support the children's good work ethic would ensure some educational success – which is really where my responsibilities with the family ended.

One day the social worker came beaming into school.

"Great news!" she said. "I think we've finally made a breakthrough with this family!"

"Good," I thought hoping they'd acquired some books or puzzles but she pressed her hands together in glee and announced,

"They've bought a new Three Piece Suite!"

Another visitor arrived, mid-lesson, to discuss her speech therapy with Libby – a newish girl with a stammer. The speech therapist spoke with such a subdued whisper that it was a wonder if any child could actually hear her. She also had concerns about 'farm children'.

"I've worked with Libby at her old school without any success at all and I'm beginning to wonder if her stammer is caused by problems at home. She lives on a farm you know," and she dipped her head knowingly. "She's 'not allowed' to do anything at all!"

Libby's stammer didn't seem to affect her much. It was more of a hesitation and didn't prevent her wanting to read aloud or relate news to the class – or to talk incessantly. I was curious about the therapist's concern though and offered to give Libby a lift home after dance-club – just for a little look.

"Hi M..M..Mummy!" Libby waved as we pulled up at the garden gate and turned to me "D..do you want to c..come and see the c..cows being milked?"

"Yes that would be lovely,"

"I..I'm n..not allowed to cross the road on my own b..but I can help you to cross," she offered and taking my hand performed a perfect Green Cross Code.

We came to a tall five-barred metal gate.

"W..we can go through here," she said leading me through, " b..but I'm not allowed through THAT one 'cos LOOK!" She laughed as she

A Bit of Helpful Advice

pointed to an enormous Hereford bull behind another metal gate.

"Daddy's already st…started milking – can you hear the machine? – we're n..not allowed right in but you can l..look through this d..door. See?"

It was a large modern milking parlour with sparkling glass jars and shiny blue steel. Two rows of black and white cows munched happily at their cake whilst a waterproofed man deftly dealt with the production end.

"L..Let's go and wait for the cows in the field," she beamed and taking my hand led me skipping into an emerald green meadow where she danced around happily picking dandelion clocks, her green-ribboned pigtails bobbing in the evening sun. I still had no clues about the cause of her stammer. She was sensibly aware of what she was not allowed to do and why – so important on a farm such as this – it certainly wasn't over-strictness.

"Here's D..Daddy!" she gleamed as he ushered the released cows into the meadow.

"You're n..not allowed to run away if they chase you – just stand still "she instructed me as her dad came over .

"H..hi," he stammered, "P..Pleased to meet you, I'm Libby's d..d..dad!"

"Is He Dyslexic?" "No, He Just Can't Read."

Another farming child in my class had major reading problems. It is clear now that he was severely dyslexic but this was in the early days of its recognition – so much so that even some teachers failed to acknowledge it. George had regular remedial help but all he could manage was recall of memorised pages which he did extremely well. However he could not read or recognise even simple words or letters or write them down in any kind of order. In other ways he was very intelligent. He could describe in detail the workings of a combine harvester, divulge the profit and loss situation of his father's farm and skilfully build or dismantle anything given to him.

"Does it matter really if he never learns to read, he's going to inherit the farm anyway!" one exasperated helper sighed.

George's father was chairman of the School Friends Committee and one weekend the staff and parents met to erect a new school shed that the Friends had purchased. George came to help because of his superior construction skills and sure enough under his supervision the 'flat-pack' was almost complete by midday. At this juncture though the adults felt it was a good time for a little liquid refreshment at The Red Lion and George was sent home to play.

The responsible adults returned just a little tipsily to put the final pieces together but without George to help they were completely befuddled.

They finally concluded that a roof piece R3 must be missing and so retreated to George's farmhouse for reviving black coffees. As they crossed the farmyard George called from high up in a tree. Looking up they saw an elaborately and expertly constructed tree-house entered by a rope ladder which reached to an enclosed platform with a smart hinged door.

"It's even got a roof look – I found some spare wood in the school field!" and he proudly pointed to the triangular roof apex clearly marked with a yellow R3.

Callum was another bright dyslexic boy, also brilliant at construction and technical drawing. After one farm visit he accurately drew and constructed a model, completely from memory, of the granary complete with corn-bins and corkscrew auger. He was seven when he arrived in the village from a very formal previous school where he'd been tested and failed frequently.

I regularly gave the children reading tests but in an informal relaxed way letting them read a text in the quiet Home Corner. Most were unaware that it WAS a test. Whilst testing another child I noticed Callum kneeling on the floor with a book and slowly edging towards us. His lips were silently mouthing words but his eyes were not on his book and I suspected that he was listening and memorising the text of the test, something he could do well. Sure enough when I tested him he was word-perfect with a reading age of 14 years. Unfortunately he scored only 6.0 years on the alternative test I gave him.

Both of these boys were bright and amiable and I hope they have now fully found their niche in a more understanding society.

Lost for Words

The child I had most concerns for wasn't officially 'special' nor under any 'official eye'. Shaun was the tiniest boy in the school even when he entered my junior class. His tiny body was as skinny as a mouse and he was also as timid as a mouse, so scared that he never spoke in school. Because however he did speak at home, he had no help from a speech therapist and was so good and quiet at school that no behaviour therapist was deemed necessary either.

To begin with he was so scared of the bigger boys in my class he refused to do games, crouching in the cloakroom corner. In the end I just put him in charge of the ball-net and he happily ran about collecting stray balls or retrieving those that flew over the hedge and got his exercise that way.

As he didn't speak though, he had no reading score to report on Parents' Evening. His parents naturally blamed his lack of progress and 'bad' home behaviour squarely on me.

"E's so naughty since e's been in your class. Yesterdee e' climbed right to the top of the tree an' wouldn't come down fer hours." (Probably felt safe up there, I thought. Just like a little sparrow.)

"I ses to 'im 'when you come down you're going straight ter bed' – an 'e still wouldn't come down. Would you believe it?"

We had several small animals in the classroom – zebra finches, guinea-pigs, frogs, tadpoles and a pair of gerbils who lived in a huge aquarium half full of sand. Shaun would stand and watch them dig and burrow for hours on end. When these two female gerbils unexpectedly gave birth I asked Shaun if he'd like to have one of the litter. He nodded pinkly and his tiny black field-mouse eyes welled up. He took it home in an old plastic fish tank with some sand and bedding and I suggested he kept it in his outhouse next to the warm kitchen.

Teachers' pay-day was Thursday. We had no 'hole in the wall' then and had to cash cheques in at the bank to get money out so on Friday lunchtimes I made the short journey in to town. There was just enough time to get there and back before afternoon school. Hurriedly grabbing my car-keys, on this particular Friday lunch-break, I noticed Shaun lingering by the gerbils after everyone had gone to lunch. Suddenly he took a huge breath – and *spoke*. It was a deep, growling voice that just wouldn't stop so on this momentous occasion I had no choice but to stay and listen.

"My gerbil likes 'is new 'ouse. I made him a little box wiv a hole an' 'e goes in an' out an' in an' out but now 'e's chewed it up so I 'ad ter make 'im anuver one wiv a tissue box and 'e goes ter sleep in the tissues an' I calls 'im Nosey cos 'is nose sticks out of the tissues an' it wiggles (he giggled) an' 'e's got a dish of water an' 'e tips it all over 'is self an' gets 'is fur all wet then 'e 'as ter dry 'imself wiv 'is front paws an' then 'e digs in the sand and the sand comes all out of the tank so can I 'ave some more sand Miss. Please?" and he finally took a breath.

Realising by now that I wouldn't make it to the bank we sat down together and I helped him write some of this story down. He managed, very slowly, to write five lines and draw a superb picture – more than he'd ever written before – and I carefully mounted it and stuck it on the wall above the gerbil tank. He stood looking proudly at his masterpiece. I would just have to manage with 75p until Monday lunchtime.

Shaun's mum came to our next Open Evening and pointed to his work on the wall.

"You 'aven't put much of Shaun's work up! I can see who your favourites are an' it ent Shaun is it?"

Walk on ... Walk on ...

We shared the use of a rattly old grey mini-bus with a neighbouring school but as it was a time of cutbacks County Officials were beginning to question whether we used it enough to justify its upkeep. Ideas for 'educational' ways to use a vehicle which could only transport half a class at a time, were hard to come by. As I came up with the only idea it was hard for the Head to dismiss it!

Several children in the village had ponies but twice as many longed for one so I thought that a horse-riding club might be popular. The mini-bus was booked and a riding school found nearby. Miss Saddler lived solely for her horses and ponies. Their wellbeing came well above that of her pupils – and marginally above her dogs – but I thought this might also develop some altruism in the children. Lessons were part riding part pony-care and as this bit qualified as 'education' I was given the go-ahead.

In the interest of equal opportunity Miss Saddler did not require her pupils to wear expensive attire. Wellies were permitted (as she used safety stirrups), old jeans and jumpers encouraged and hard hats could be borrowed from an empty galvanised water tank full of old lost property. Willow riding crops were collected each lesson from her nearby osier bed.

After a short introduction to the ponies and a long discourse about the pony's needs the lesson began at a snail's pace around the indoor ménage.

The bored ponies, having repeated the lessons for yonks, anticipated every instruction before they were uttered , heightening the children's sense of achievement. Miss Saddler must have known that behind her back each pony was stopping for a mouthful at the hay-net.

"Do NOT let your ponies stop and eat!" she hailed. "HANDS down, HEELS down, SIT UP and WALK ON!"

Libby had a pretty grey Welsh and kept leaning forward and hugging its mane which didn't help with its manoeuvrability. Rupert's feet stuck out at right angles matching his red-beacon ears and Callum battled earnestly with lazy Goldie who kept cutting across the ménage home to her stall. Bouncer didn't move at all – let alone bounce.

"What a ramshackle lot!" shouted Miss Saddler from the centre, "Tighten those reins, prepare to TROT and TROT ON!"

As the ponies pre-empted the trot on the 'prepare' word they took all the children by surprise and two backward-somersaulted off. Feet and reins flopped everywhere as the remainder earnestly grabbed hold of their saddles.

"NEVER NEVER hold the saddle!" Miss Saddler shrieked.

"Grab the mane! Rupert pull the reins, pull the reins!" she urged unsuccessfully. "Pull the reins NOW Rupert before Paddy... Oh dear... CATCH THAT PONY!" she shouted down the lane.

"You children MUST remember to latch the door properly," she said later after first dusting Paddy and then Rupert down. "Perhaps now I should walk round with each of you and make sure you can

52 LITTLE GREEN SHOOTS

do a proper HALT. Walk on!" but as she concentrated on Melissa, Conker – a naughty black pony conveying Joseph – decided he'd like a taste of the action as well and trotted over to the door. Expertly taking the latch in his teeth he opened the door and trotted out to the inviting grass in the orchard depositing Joseph halfway there.

Rupert and Joseph decided not to go there again. Bicycles, they felt, were a much safer option.

For a few children though these lessons were the start of a lifetime passion, some going on to competitive riding, others to keeping show ponies and some just riding for pleasure.

"You have a lot to answer for," a very cash-strapped mother said to me some years later at a horse show.

Miss Saddler's riding school held several little leading-rein gymkhanas and the children were able to borrow her ponies to take part.

These events were aimed at 'Confidence Building Through Friendly Competition' – a point lost on the parents attached to the end of the leading reins. There were mug-races, musical-sacks and potato-races where wayward hooves sent the potato bucket flying into the unwary spectators. In the Handy Pony (a kind of obstacle race) Paddy stopped to eat all the sugar lumps at the tea table much to Lindsay's embarrassment and then old Bouncer finally woke up and galloped round the Clear Round ring – a simple circle of very low jumps designed I suspect to test the agility of the leading mums rather than pony or mount. Bouncer enjoyed this Grand National so much that whilst we were all engrossed in admiring the rosettes afterwards, he chewed through his leading rein and trotted back to the Clear Round ring giving his traumatised rider three free rounds – and an extra 'Bravery' rosette.

Eggs is Eggs

It was fashionable then, in Primary Education, to operate an 'Integrated Day'. This involved several small groups of children working on different subjects all at the same time and all related to the main topic. This grossly irritated the more traditional parents who preferred 'proper subject timetables' but the method does seem to be re-emerging as primary schools have over-concentrated on only the 'examined' core subjects.

The coming of Easter annually gifted us the topic of 'Eggs'. We borrowed a small incubator to hatch some chicks and in the three waiting weeks collected and worked on a variety of eggs – ants' eggs, frogspawn, butterfly eggs but mostly hens' eggs. The eggs arrived daily (a necessity with Gary's breakage rate) in boxes of half dozens, dozens and grosses immediately offering practical activities with 2x 3x 6x and 12x tables. The discarded boxes were then carefully crafted into turtles and tortoises. Other maths lessons developed into weighing, measuring and often breaking eggs – but even broken eggs provided an exciting science lesson.

"How much weight will it hold before it breaks?" or "How high will it drop from before it smashes?" was the ultimate favourite.

In art they made paper-maché Humpty-Dumpties around inflated balloons and compared waist circumferences to find the greediest Humpty. Much to the girls' distress a few boys tested 'how far Humpty could fall from before he broke?' on the playground walls.

Their written work culminated in some outstanding and very sensitive accounts of what it would feel like to be a chick hatching from an egg just as our real chicks hatched and dried into yellow powder puffs.

"Ah!" and "Ooh!" the enthralled faces cooed.

During the last two days before one Easter holiday I succumbed to a heavy cold and stayed at home leaving detailed instructions for 'Decorated Eggs' with my class-room assistant.

The children blew the eggs then filled them with Plaster of Paris using an icing syringe. When fully set they painted them with appropriate Easter symbols like daffodils, chicks or crosses – or in Roy's case, lorries.

On the first day of the holiday there was a knock at my door and Tina, unwrapping her paint-strewn fingers, presented me with a lovingly hand-painted egg. With utmost reverence we displayed it on the warm mantelpiece.

Over the course of the holidays a strange sulphury smell began to pervade the house. Living near several farms I assumed it to be a temporary natural occurrence but the smell worsened. Armed with a hanky-covered nose I searched the cupboards, under cushions and under chairs finally tracking down the guilty offender – Tina's now less-than-gaudy green tinged egg.

"Your egg looked beautiful Tina. Was it the one you did at school?"

"No. My mum boiled it for breakfast but she said it smelt funny and threw it out so I found it later and painted it specially for you."

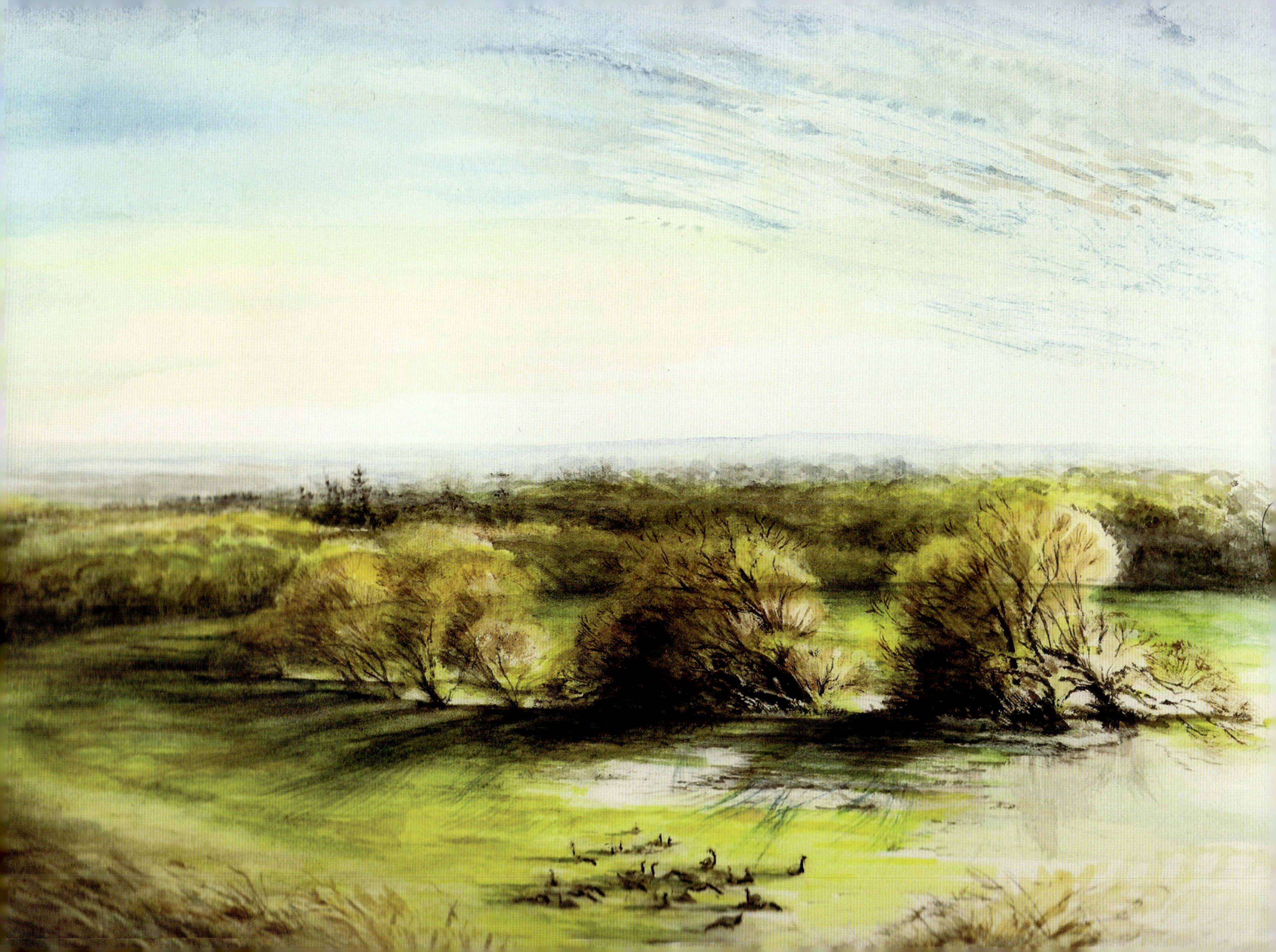

Summer Term

Cricket is Cricket

The cuckoos of early summer heralded in the ceremonial opening of the huge canvas cricket bag. Eager boys dragged it out of the old stone cupboard and dusted off the clingy grey cobwebs before releasing the nostalgic musty smell of leather and linseed. With three boys clutching each handle the bag struggled up the steps to the field where Nigel's dad had meticulously mown a velvet green square with his old Suffolk Punch cylinder mower.

From now until term ended, every lunch-time the boys (and some girls) were coached by our Head Teacher in the glorious game of cricket. There were no lightweight balls and plastic cricket bats here. This was the real thing and even the tiniest boys were padded up to face a hard leather ball with an unwieldy willow bat.

They learnt the game slowly but knowledgably over the course of their four junior years, beginning as fielders and progressing over the years to slips, wicket-keepers and bowlers. The only slight rule-bend was that every batsman batted only two whole overs (an 'out' being a minus run) otherwise Nigel would still have been 'not out' at the end of his primary school career. It was quietly but seriously competitive with scores meticulously recorded and little awards presented at the end of term.

At the first summer term staff meeting the Head surprisingly and unexpectedly announced,

"I don't think competitive sport is right for a primary school. I'm thinking in particular about Sports Day. There's far too much competitiveness involved, especially amongst the parents".

The rest of the staff sat dumbfounded whilst an innocent visiting student piped up,

"Well you could just not invite the parents," quite underestimating the importance of this social occasion – a chance to take a day off work, don dresses and summer hats, sample home-made cream teas and generally gossip and reminisce. Sometimes they would even watch the races.

"Well – what about making little teams, each doing a shuttle relay with different kinds of games skills?"

Now ideas came thick and fast and the Head jotted down notes excitedly. Soon preparations for a new 'Summer Sports Family Day' were nearly complete. The whole school, of around 100, would be sorted into ten groups of mixed age and ability with a top junior group-leader. These groups would rotate around simple skills – such as ball in the hoop, bean-bag in a bucket, in a relay system – just like Pony Club games in fact! A parent scorer on each game would jot down 'hits' This was controversial as it hinted of competition but allowed for purposes of 'incentive'! The Head had not yet decided what to do with these 'scores'.

Last of all, but most important were the 'hot weather preparations'; bottles of water and sun-creams, shady parasols for heat retreat and of prime importance the half-time cooling ice-lollies kindly donated by the village shop.

Consequently the day dawned cold, grey and overcast and remained so. One hundred teeth-chattering, goose-bumped T-shirted children trotted out onto the cold, dank field and formed orderly lines by the appointed starting game. In the centre of this large circle was Mrs Broome, our proudly appointed timekeeper, bell-ringer and whistle-blower who sat under a parasol and, oddly, behind an office desk. It was strangely reminiscent of a scene from 'Monty Python'. The whistle was the signal to stop the game and move on and the bell to start the next. As this was in sharp contrast to playground procedure the first two games began under a kerfuffle of confusion further confounded by Tina leading her group anti-clockwise instead of clockwise.

Soon the children shivered to a halt at half-time and sat waiting for their cooling and refreshing ice lollies.

"I thought I'd keep them overnight in my cold store so's they wouldn't melt but they've gone a bit too 'ard," the village shopkeeper informed us handing out rock-hard lumps of frost-covered ice to purple-blue fingers. Alexander howled as he bit into his,

"Miss … Miss ... my toof's come out!" so he was sent for a 'rinse' in the toilets.

"Perhaps it's better just to lick them – look at those lovely bright colours when you've licked the frost off," I said ominously.

"Miss … Miss ... Roy's tongue's got stuck to 'is lolly!"
An inspection after separation revealed a large red blister.
"Bobby's lips 'ave stuck togever Miss an' 'e can't speak!"
"Good thing," muttered his mum.

As the five-minute break broke the ten minute barrier, headway was finally made through the frost-crusted ices to reveal a rainbow of fluorescent food colourings prompting lipstick comparisons amongst the girls.

"My mouth's red."
"Mine's green!"
"My lips are orange!"

"My lips are sealed," a mum muttered, then a little side competition began amongst the boys to see who could paint the most ice-lolly on their faces. We reformed into lines of little Red Indians. The re-start was restarted with a whistle and then restarted again with the correct signal. One particular game seemed to go on forever and the children started to get a little 'unfocused' with the rather unchallenging tasks. The Head's loudhailer hailed loudly towards centre field.

"Mrs Broome! Mrs Broome! Are you awake? Time's up I think," and 100 rainbow faces turned to face the little hypothermic huddle of Mrs Broome hidden in two woolly cardigans. She was revived with hot tea whilst the children grew more and more unsettled and bluntly naughty, requiring responsible adults and teachers to patrol and pick a team to 'manage'.

I noticed that my team's scores were particularly high, uniquely filling a second page so I observed closely. Stanley, the team leader, was rather overenthusiastically helping the little ones with an occasional push and shove where he deemed it worthwhile.

"Miss I dowanna play anymore," an infant whimpered, snatching my hand. Then I noticed that Alistair and his sister Alice were ALWAYS at the back of the line. Each time a finishing performer joined the end they would feign loose laces or lazy socks and surreptitiously fall to the back again. They didn't perform any tasks at all and Stanley was quite happy to concentrate on his faster ones anyway.

No wonder their scores were so good.

Alistair was extremely gifted academically but resisted anything that involved bodily movement and his shape rather reflected this. Due to this lethargy he was constantly cold and wore a woolly duffle-coat everywhere. Deprived of this necessary garment today he was clearly suffering withdrawal symptoms.

"This is all far too trivial in my opinion," he said crossly to me "and it's having a detrimental effect up on my sister's well-being. She is uncharacteristically over-agitated," as indeed was the whole school. Little niggles began to erupt.

"Tony DON'T pull Sasha's hair please !"

"I never Miss. I was strokin' it. An' my finger accidentally got stuck to my fumb!"

At last the full-time whistle blew and the school gathered around Mrs Broome's office desk and her slightly drooping parasol. The Head hushed them and made his 'well done everyone you've all worked hard and deserve a clap' speech but then embarked upon an unexpected announcement.

"Although today was NOT about competition but just about 'family fun' and 'helping each other' I have asked Mrs Broome, just out of interest, to tot-up the scores."

Alistair slowly raised his hand.

"As that may take considerable time might I be permitted to assist you with the calculations?"

The Head agreed eagerly as fidgeting and shivering increased but just as Alistair announced,

"Results are now in and Here are the Scores … in No Particular Order …" little Alexander emerged crying from the school toilets. He'd been inadvertently overlooked since his tooth fell out at half-time.

"I've lost my toof down the toilet – can you come and find it for the toof fairy?" he sobbed.

The Head promised that the Tooth Fairy would definitely be able to find it herself and quickly read out Alistair's carefully calculated results.

"… and so, although this was not really a competition, would the winning team, which was Stanley's, come and get their awards!"

Stanley proudly led his team up whilst the Head delved deep into a box hidden in the office desk. He pulled out eleven hideously shiny gold medals hanging on eleven slightly frayed ribbons and ceremoniously adorned the team. The medals were obviously superfluous to a previous football tournament as they were each embossed with a pair of boots but they were proudly worn and jealously coveted. The Head continued, despite catching our critical eyes,

"As I had eleven medals I was going to award the last one to 'the Most Helpful Pupil' but he's already got one so I'm sure you'll agree that Mrs Broome deserves this medal for her excellent timekeeping."

Mrs Broome graciously accepted her medal and began a little speech,

"I'd like to thank my husband …"

"No time Mrs Broome," said the Head ushering her away. She returned to her desk and sat tearfully admiring her reward, quite oblivious to the drooping parasol which slowly sank down and enveloped her completely.

"So, finally, I have found another prize for 'the most helpful pupil' who was Alistair, as he's been so kind to his sister Alice today."

A rather embarrassed Alistair went up to receive a foil-wrapped chocolate reindeer left over from the Christmas Bazaar.

"Well here's one creature that might appreciate this weather," he muttered.

The day after our Summer Sports Family Day dawned bright, sunny and hot as 'days after' tend to do.

"On the whole a very successful day I think!" pronounced the ever-optimistic Head.

"Perhaps leaving out the e-numbers in the lollies might make it even

> Dear Toof fairy
> I lost my toof down the school boys toylet
> plees can I have 50p
> from Alexander.

more successful," added the Deputy "– fifteen headaches and three night-terrors were reported" she frowned.

"And IF it's really meant to be non-competitive, NO shiny medals – or other prizes?" I suggested. The Head coughed in embarrassment.

"I think you are to be congratulated Headmaster," the visiting vicar and governor spluttered through an iced bun, "and I think we should now embrace your policy right across the board and make ALL physical education in the school non-competitive. We should just teach skills and abandon all competition – including football and cricket matches. Well done Sir!"

The Head went a little pale and his jaw silently dropped.

"But … not cricket!"

He swallowed as a small tear moistened his cheek

"You can't change cricket. Cricket … is cricket."

Playground Games

The non-competitive sport debate continues to this day but whatever policy currently pervaded, the playground games remained seriously competitive with no apparent detrimental affect on the participating children. Their rules were made and obeyed without question and required no adult referee. The winners won and the losers lost and that was that. Then they played it again.

"Play next playtime?" were the shouts at the bell.

The craze amongst the girls then was Norwegian Skipping, based upon several metres of knicker-elastic stretched into an oblong between two facing pairs of legs. The 'in' girl performed an elaborate series of jumps and twists within the elastic which moved higher up the legs as performance improved, "kneesie" being the highest and "footsie" lowest. No-one was traumatised when they were 'out' or sneered when they won. They just got on with it.

The boys' football was equally competitive but the teams organically evolved as circumstances changed. If you scored too many goals you had to change sides to make the game fairer or five infants would swap for two juniors to balance the sides.

The most keenly-fought game of all never even saw a winning team because it went on into eternity. It was a sprint shuttle relay with two teams either ends of the playground criss-crossing ends and exchanging a stick or stone. Children would join in or leave the line as the mood took them so team numbers were always very 'liquid'. Everyone felt they were a winner because there was always an opposing runner behind them in the sequence. It carried on all summer from one playtime to the next and had no beginning, no end and no winning team, but what exhilarating fun it was to run as fast as you could and believe you were an Olympic Champion.

With our non-competitive sports policy were we denying each child the chance to perform to their best?

A Fallen Idol

One summer evening I finally met the last of Jo's siblings. He arrived at the farm in a brilliant flash of gold (a yellow Ford Capri) skidding noisily to a halt somewhere behind the garden fence. Another dramatic entrance followed as he burst into the kitchen.

"Ta-da! Your prince returns Mother dear!" pranced a relatively good-looking young male.

"Oh hello Jack dear – are you staying for supper?"

"Mother," he said flexing his muscles before the mirror, "I'm going straight out. How can I deprive the world any longer of this beautiful Adonis?"

"Hm."

On his way out after a meticulously long beauty-bath that used the whole tank-full of hot water he added,

"By the way Mother, I should get and mend your fences, they're all rotten."

"Cheek!" retorted Annie "Nothing wrong with OUR fences."

The following morning there was some sort of hassle with the hens. Annie's favourite speckled hen lay exhausted on the drive, panting slowly with an open beak and others were refusing to eat or lay any eggs.

"Must be that fox. Cheeky thing stole my best white hen yesterday – right under my nose!" squawked Annie and the hens squawked back. As she sympathetically picked up the speckled one it opened its beak and with a very polite and apologetic 'chicken burp' burped out several bright green peas! Sympathy now dispelled, Annie threw the hen back down, "Blasted hens! They've been in MY garden, stealing MY peas!"

Annie was still rather disgruntled when Jack returned at lunchtime – looking a little less Adonis-like .

"There's NOTHING for lunch, no eggs and no vegetables," she stated. "The hens haven't laid any eggs because they've got into the garden and got sick eating all my vegetables," she grunted. "You were right about the fence dear, there was a great big hole in it."

"I told you to get and mend the fence Mother…you can have the fence-post back if you like, it's stuck in my radiator grill."

Pastures New

My cold-toed evenings in the mouse-house came to an end when I was offered a cottage on the nearby country estate. As it was an agriculture-tied cottage one condition of my residency was that I should work an hour or two on the farm at the weekend. Fred the farmer was on the verge of retirement and all his fields had been ploughed up for cereal growing but he still had a few young bullocks to finish in his covered yard.

"Praps of a Sunday when my man's 'off' you could feed and litter them down. I's too old now. I'll get my man to put the hay and straw on the trailer so's you just have to drive the tractor straight round – you won' 'ave ter reverse it!" he chuckled. The tractor driving turned out to be the easiest bit. I'd expected his 'young' bullocks to be a bit smaller than the flaring nostrils which stampeded towards me. Being a little green at this, I carried the straw in first – only to have to beat a hasty retreat over the rails as they tossed and kicked the bale in a bovine version of 'keepy uppy'. I left them to it and carried in the hay only just managing to escape a second stampede.

"Next time," I said to myself "throw the hay over first then whilst they're busy eating, toss in the straw." I noticed Fred amusingly watching from his garden, resting his chin on his stick.

Applying my new method the following week I had more success but again noticed Fred watching, although he pretended to be dead-heading his roses.

On the third Sunday he wandered over and poked a bullock on the rump with his old hazel stick.

"Not finished yet," he said, referring I think to the bullock. Then he cleared his throat and announced,

"I don't think you'd better do this anymore. It's getting a bit too risky."

"Oh no. It's fine now I've sussed out how to occupy them with the hay first," I pleaded.

"Well actually I wasn't thinkin' about your safety, I was just a bit concerned you might scratch my new tractor on that gate post."

Fred wasn't the only one concerned about my competence. There was always a steady flow of estate workers dawdling past my garden on their way home and they each stopped to comment on something.

"Yer can't plant them cabbages there! They'll not grow there!"

"Yer can't burn that wood on yer fire – that's pinewood."

"Yer'll set fire ter chimney then us'll ALL burn down."

"Young gals shouldna live on their own – 'tent safe."

"You wants ter find a nice flat in town."

"Country ways ent fer young lasses like yoos."

Then much to their satisfaction a little accident confirmed their predictions. I'd set to work in the garden to clear a large patch of nettles and caught my thumb on some hidden broken glass. It looked like just a small triangular scratch until I turned my thumb downwards and the small triangle also flapped downwards. Several rounds of kitchen roll later I decided I needed assistance so reluctantly ventured out into the lane holding up a large red and white football. Angie the Farm and Estate Secretary had cheerily related to me that week how she had passed her First Aid exam and was now the 'Official Estate First Aider' so I headed for her office. It was pay-day so a large captive audience was there waiting to collect their wage-packets.

"Oh Lor," Angie said, visibly paling when she saw my sodden bandage, "What do I do now?"

"I think stitches are required – could you drive me to the cottage hospital please!"

"Okay," she said sitting down and fanning her ashen face with a brown wage packet, "But I'll have to hand out all their wages first. Sit there."

We were not short of advice as one by one the men collected their wages and donated helpful comments,

"You warnts ter 'old it up so's the blood washes all the muck out."

"It'll go sceptical, else."

"Ar, mine did that."

"My missus did that cookin' my supper. Spoilt the 'ole lot."

"Thas what 'appens when young lasses lives on their own."

"You cud bleed ter death out 'ere an no-one ud know."

"Ole Fred, 'e said a young lass could never clear them nettles an' yer never did, did yer?"

"That were a greenhouse under them nettles, storm of '72 blew it away, jus' left glass. I coulda told yer there was glass in them nettles."

"I wish you had," I thought.

At last Angie was ready, bundling me into her car after first placing a towel on the seat and handing me another.

"Wrap it in that, I don't want to touch it."

We got to the cottage hospital some seven miles away and she parked under the pretty rose-lined window.

"I won't come in," she said nervously, "I can't stand hospitals," so holding the giant red football aloft I negotiated the doors with my foot. The duty doctor was young and enthusiastic explaining the anatomy of my thumb in unnecessary detail.

"Angie's one of your neighbours then!" he exclaimed as I gave my address," I've just passed her on the First Aider's Test."

"Yes – she's waiting out there, under the window."

"Oh great!" he said striding over and leaning out precariously, "Angie! Hi! Would you like to further your First Aid knowledge and help me do the stitches?"

"Oh no!" replied Angie "I can't stand the sight of blood!"

Dancing Queen

Many of our parents volunteered to run school clubs and one of the most popular was the Country Dancing. It was held during summer term and culminated in a performance at the school fête. This particular year a professionally trained dancer, Mrs Tapper, had offered to teach some new and rather more advanced dances. Coloured ribbons and hoops were to be involved so there were lots of volunteering children and playground practices commenced.

All was not however going quite to plan. Cries of,

"Oh Tina!"

"Ieee Naa."

"Left turn Tina – No LEFT!" wafted in through the schoolroom windows with increasing exasperation. Poor Tina could not get her tiny feet to go either in the right direction or the right order. She was desperate to take part and had already shown me her chosen costume – a frilly pink tucked bridesmaid's dress handed down by her step-sister … but we all knew the dance would end in disaster if she did.

Mrs Tapper had an idea. She announced to the dancers,

"This year we are going to have a Queen of the Dance who will lead in the dancers and then oversee them from a special throne, decorated with beautiful flowers."

"Ooo!"

"Me Miss me!"

"Can it be me please?"

Mrs Tapper signalled for silence and explained.

"We are going to put names in a hat and the name that is picked out will be Queen."

"Do we all have to put names in Miss – I don't wanna be a Queen?" Gary asked worriedly.

"Well, you could be a handsome Prince?"

"Neh," Gary jeered, after careful thought.

At the next practice they all gathered around a large top-hat (from Mrs Tapper's past glories on the stage) and Gary was chosen to 'pick'.

"TINA. It says 'Tina' Miss."

Tina was elated and couldn't stop grinning.

"I can still wear my bridesmaid dress. It looks just like the Queen's dress!"

"Well that was a bit of luck!" I sighed to Mrs Tapper afterwards.

"Not really. ALL the names in the hat said 'Tina'."

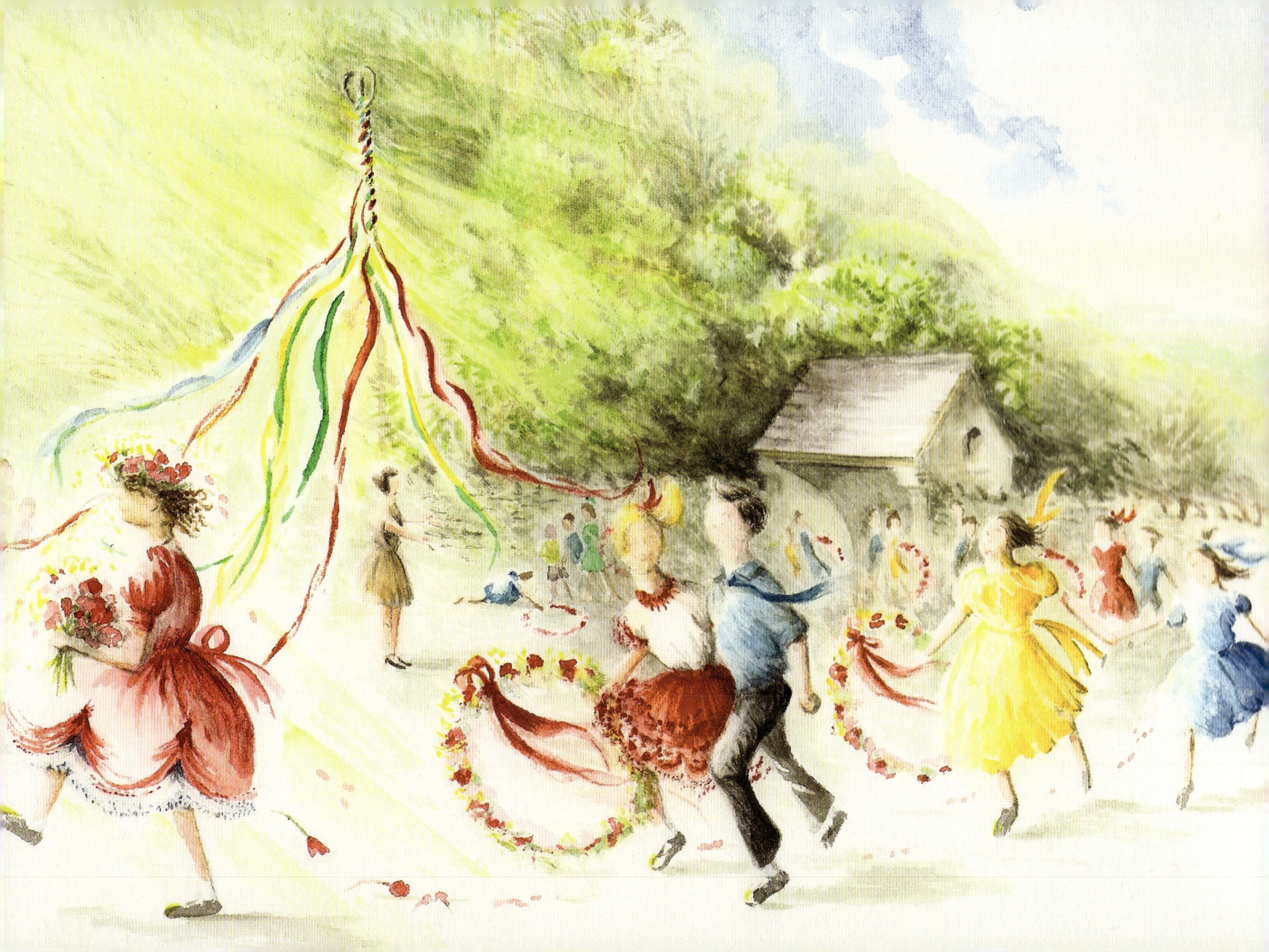

Tigger was Very Bouncy

As a housewarming present my Headmaster kindly gave me a kitten. He'd been looking for a home for his unwanted litter and had one kitten left. I was reluctant to accept it at first but after a dramatic plea about its imminent anaesthesia, I succumbed.

I didn't want to leave it on its own in the cottage all day – partly for its own sake but also because after only one hour of residence it had managed to wreck the place, toppling china off the dresser, pulling down curtains and unravelling a particularly nice hand-woven cushion – a gift from a Norwegian exchange visit.

The kitten christened itself, becoming 'Tigger' not because of its prominent black stripes but because it was Very Bouncy.

I concluded that the best place for it to be Very Bouncy was in my large outhouse so during my working day Tigger went to his playschool of suspended cotton-reels, rattles, bells, balls and other educational toys. He pined a bit when I left him but when I returned he was always curled up asleep in an exhausted, contented ball of fur.

I made up for this abandonment with boisterous play in the evenings but he showed increasingly more preference for a fireside sleep.

"Mrs Steele's got a new cat," Angie imparted passing my garden as I played with Tigger. "She was telling me how it goes on walks with her and Nipper – strange how that vicious dog gets on with a cat – they even share a bed!"

Returning home one evening I found the outhouse door ajar and Tigger missing. Milk left outside for it was left untouched and I feared the worst. Angie called by as I refilled the saucer.

"Mrs Steele's not very well. You couldn't take her dog out for a walk could you? – she asked me to, but I am scared of dogs." Dutifully I knocked on Mrs Steele's door, next but one to mine.

"Come in Angie dear!" she sang but upon seeing me enter she became rather anxious, pulling up her rug around her neck and shaking. I tried to reassure her.

"Hello – Angie is a bit busy so I've come to take Nipper out for you."

"Oh dear, oh dear," she said trembling, "I'm so, so sorry," and she pointed to her sleeping dog, contentedly curled up with Tigger.

"I heard your kitten pining in the outhouse so I brought it home to play with Nipper – just for a little while. I normally take it back before you come home but I've felt so ill I couldn't move – I'm so sorry."

Tigger and Nipper looked so happy together that I thought it would be a shame to part them. I told Mrs Steele that hers was a far better home than mine for a kitten and so she could keep it.

A few days later Angie passed by on her way to the Post Office,

"Mrs Steele's kitten looks JUST Like yours," she commented "Are they from the same litter?"

"They are actually – just the same," I replied .

Hooper's Hedgerow

The agreeable weather of the Summer Term invited out my own special subject, Environmental Science. Currently (2010) absent from English Primary Schools, Environmental Science was a combination of natural science, geography and history coordinated with writing, artwork and practical maths. I think it's the 'coordination' which puts the present tick-box authorities off! I hope it returns to the curriculum.

We had embarked upon a Hedgerow Study and were aiming to date our historic playing field boundary hedge through multi-subject tasks. Fellow teachers may be familiar with 'Hooper's Hedgerow Theory' where basically for every 100 metres of hedge each different tree species represents 100 years of hedge age. For the children it would involve measuring out ten 10-metre sections of hedge, drawing, identifying and mapping different species using reference books and finally writing up their findings. It involved nearly every school subject and was NOT as some parents described it, 'a day out in the fields'.

A day after the first session Jane's mother appeared in school with a concerned expression and an equally concerned Jane attached.

"She's allergict to the hedge!" she frowned pointing to a row of tiny red insect bites on Jane's leg. "I'm not having her wasting her time in that hedge anymore. Its full of creepy–crawlies and it's DIRTY!" she sneered. "I want her to stay inside and do PROPER work!"

That lunchtime Jane and Sasha sat happily in the field, next to the hedge, making an enormous daisy-chain. They enlisted four more children to help them carry it in to show the class. We counted 180 daisies and it measured just over 9 metres. 'That's 20 daisies in each metre,' we calculated and they laid it down in a huge 9-metre circle and measured it across the diameter. It was about 3 metres. 'The circumference is three times as big as the diameter', we eventually concluded (3.142 times to be exact and thus they were introduced to π).

For the afternoon Jane went into the top junior class with her maths workbook and stared longingly as we trooped out to the hedge. On the way there Sasha showed me an itchy row of little red insect bites on her leg.

"We always get bitten by ants when we pick daisies," she said "but we don't care."

Jane nearly didn't take part in our pond-study either. After the ant-affair, for the pond visit I suggested that the children wear trousers, or shorts with wellies as extra protection. In popped Jane's mother again.

"Jane can't go pond-dipping. She hasn't got any wellies because she doesn't go out in the wet."

"Could she wear old shoes with trousers?" I ventured.

"None of MY girls EVER wears trousers!"

In the end Jane persuaded her mum to look through a circulating 'posh' clothes catalogue for some 'nice girl's trousers'. She reluctantly purchased a smart tartan pair explaining to her neighbours "They're NOT trousers they're 'Ladies Tailored Slacks'"

They came in very useful for picking daisies.

The Giant Yellow Monster

My tiny new cottage had a kitchen and living room downstairs and bedroom and spare for a study/studio upstairs. The kitchen had fitted hand-made cupboards and a cooker but no fridge.

"I knows just the thing," said Fred the landlord, then added sadly, "we won't be needin' it with no more milkers ... Anyway I'll send it round on the sack-cart with my man."

My new fridge arrived on a creaking sack-cart steadied by two men. It was too big to go through the back door so was squeezed in with encouragement through the front. When placed on the only spare floor space in the kitchen we found we couldn't open the back door. We had no choice but to stand it in the doorway between the two rooms where we'd just had to remove the door, leaving barely 6 inches 'squeeze-past' space. It was a giant yellow monster, higher than I could reach, with thick, fat sides – and it hummed a very irritating hum.

Visitors to the cottage acquired a 'front door' or 'back door' status – back for food- and drink-related visits and front for formal or fireside visits. As my table was in the front room it was easier to eat or drink standing up in the kitchen. The fridge held six times the amount of food I needed and the irritating hum reverberated all over the cottage. It would have to go – but I couldn't let Fred know and hurt his feelings.

The Friends of the School were raising money for new games equipment and the Head announced a forthcoming 50/50 auction in the village hall just before half-term holiday.

" Why don't you sell that custard-yellow fridge?" he suggested having recently failed to negotiate the narrow gap between my kitchen and the front room, whilst carrying a hot coffee.

So that Fred would never know, the old yellow monster was loaded onto Roy's dad's truck after dark and taken to the village hall. I had arranged a trip back home so couldn't attend the auction but patted the fridge and wished it well in its new home.

Returning later in the holiday I found a note from the Parish Council pushed under the door. It stated that 'Fly-tipping was a fine-able offence' and asked me to remove my rubbish from their land. I thought it was a mistake or referred to a previous tenant but back at school was greeted by a delegation from the 'Friends' committee.

"Your fridge is STILL on the Parish Council Playing Field."

"It's been there all school holiday. Someone could easily get trapped inside. A child might DIE!"

"It can't stay there anyway – it's the Bowls Captain's parking space," added the Bowls Club secretary.

"It was supposed to have been sold in the auction," I explained defensively.

"Well, it was far too big to get in the hall so they left it in the field. Everyone had to go outside to bid for it. But nobody did bid. Unsold items have to be removed. Didn't you know that?" a haughty 'Friend' huffed.

Well I certainly didn't want it back again. In the end Gary's dad took it away (in 'is van). I hope it's now humming away happily in a much larger home but I suspect it was worth more to Gary's dad as scrap.

A couple of weeks later Fred called round to the cottage with his man to put some doors on my garage,

"Else it'll go the way of the greenhouse in the great storm of '72." He glared quizzically at the empty space in the kitchen.

"I'm sorry" I explained kindly "but I've ordered a slightly smaller fridge."

"That's alright, I don't know why you wanted that thing in the first place – ugly great monster".

You Can't Win Them All

Matthew was a very bright boy with a dry sense of humour. He could read well and was exceptionally good at maths, particularly mental arithmetic. What he did not display though was any form of creativity. His stories were matter-of-fact and his paintings often just black lines or splodges – his favourite colour. He could not, in fact, get anything tidily down on paper and his illegible handwriting was beginning to give his parents and me some concern. There were no obvious hindrances to explain his curiously malformed stick letters, he wrote with his right hand and his eyesight was fine but his script was always as follows:

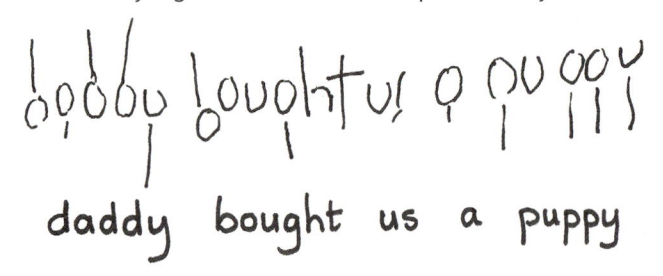

bobby boughtus a pu ppy

daddy bought us a puppy

He had been given tracing patterns, writing exercises and a specially purchased (costly) stencil set but when his hand was let loose again it just wrote in wobbly sticks. His mother blamed me.

"I really blame you. It's the school's responsibility to teach him to write properly. We are beginning to look at OTHER schools," she threatened but I did keep on trying.

One afternoon my class went onto the field where I introduced them to a game of 'quick rounders'. One team stood in a large circle with the bowler (me) in the middle. The batting team faced me in the usual way and could score a 'rounder' by running right round the outside of the circle before the ball could be thrown around it. With a round flat bat and large ball it was weighted in favour of batsmen to ensure everyone's success. As further incentive I offered an extra rounder to anyone who could hit a 'boundary'. Matthew was last to bat and carefully eyed up the distant hedge. He then picked up the bat in his left hand and slogged the ball way over the boundary.

"Bonus Rounder!" he yelled.

"Try that again Matthew", I urged "just to rule out luck," but he successfully swiped twice more in a comfortable kack-handed grip. Matthew was LEFT–HANDED.

That night I couldn't sleep, trying to remember half-listened-to lectures about the crossover of left and right brain hemispheres – was it that right-handers were more analytical, left-handers creative? Did that mean that Matthew might have a creative streak waiting to burst forth. Surely at least now I could teach him to write legibly. The following day I sought out his mother, eager with my news.

"Left-handed?" she gasped as if it was an affliction "No. NO he's ALWAYS been right handed."

"Perhaps that was because he thought it was the correct hand to use. He does like to be correct. I'd be happy to give him extra lessons to develop his left hand and I'm sure handwriting will improve."

"I don't think so," she politely refused and departed.

Sadly Matthew transferred to a neighbouring school. His mother is

You Can't Win Them All

now a professional artist and Matthew does her accounts for her, being a fully qualified Chartered Accountant. He still has appalling handwriting.

There were always a few children who left our school at the age of seven or eight to go into private education 'because that's what all our family do'. The parents often elaborated with other explanations or apologies.

"I took the day off specially to watch Melissa on Sports Day and you didn't have any hurdles! All schools do hurdles – I always won the hurdles," said one father on Open Evening, "… and Marcus is SIX now and doesn't even know where Delhi is on a map. So we're sending them both to schools where they do PROPER sport and PROPER geography … And Prep."

Edward's father then announced that Edward would soon be joining his brother at boarding school, politely adding,

"I'm really impressed with what you do here – the way you get them writing so well, so early, it's astonishing."

"Oh thank you … so why do you want him to leave?"

"Well. It's for the cricket really,"

"But we play cricket here – every day of summer term,"

"Yes, but you know – proper cricket with whites and caps and everything."

The twins' mother then piped up to declare their imminent departure.

"I agree. When the twins' brother left here he was so far ahead of his fellow boarders that he wasted a whole year before they caught up. Rupert though, won't be going until he's had a little operation to pin his ears back – they're such bullies there, they're sure to tease him about his giant red beacons!"

"What about Lindsay – the twins are almost inseparable?" I enquired, concerned.

"Oh we haven't found her anywhere yet – we're hoping to put her en route between the boys' school and our weekend place."

Melissa went on to a private school where they did tennis, but no hurdles, while her younger brother Marcus travelled a daily 40-mile round journey to prep school.

Rupert, who used to write pages of fantastically imaginative stories – and whom I thought might become a journalist is now 'something in finance' in the City but I have never heard any news of his twin sister.

I don't think Edward ever became a famous cricketer but perhaps you know otherwise.

A Question of Trust

The Top Junior Leavers were to have a special leavers' treat, a visit to a National Trust historic property within a pretty chocolate-box village. I was invited to help while my class doubled-up grudgingly with the infants.

To ensure absolute best behaviour the elated leavers were divided into small controllable groups – group size diminishing in opposition to the degree of control deemed necessary. I was assigned to the smallest group, William, Stanley and Adam.

To make the treat 'educational', proposed tasks had been set out on printed sheets attached to a board with a massive bulldog clip. Purely in the interests of education Stanley sought to discover whether his clip would attach to various items of girls' clothing. Having satisfied this curiosity he sought to discover whether it might hurt – just a little – if attached as well to the skin beneath.

My group – minus Stanley's bulldog clip – headed down into the ancient kitchens of the old house. We had decided to 'rotate' the groups around tasks to minimise their impact on this pristine village.

Here in the kitchens I discovered William's writing was so painstakingly slow he would never have time to complete the sheets. Instead I suggested he drew something he found interesting. He drew the giant roasting spit adding a ghoulishly spiked pink pig seemingly suffering a live roasting. Adam then turned out to be severely dyslexic so I read out the questions to him and he drew pictures for his answers. His detailed drawings were outstanding.

"That ent fair Miss," moaned Stanley. "They gets ter draw an I as ter work."

"That's life Stanley."

The basement kitchen began to get chilly so we rotated to our next task in the village church. As we approached the churchyard we noticed a group of girls crying and in some distress whilst their poor parent-helper was being prodded in the shoulder by a large elderly lady and her small companion.

"We are going to report you and your school to the Church Authorities. Did you even ask permission to go in OUR church – I think NOT!" her knobbly finger poked. Our helper defended herself admirably.

"Nobody needs permission to enter a church – a church is open to everyone – that's what church is about," she calmly stated. The small elderly companion then joined in with a broadside attack.

"We don't want their sticky fingers all over the brasses AND they were walking over the tombstones. They have NO respect. Those people in there are DEAD you know!"

This brought horror and disgust to the innocent girls who ran straight away back to the waiting coach. My group beat a hasty retreat back to the sanctity of the National Trust gardens where we descended a stone-walled terrace of cascading white rambler roses, exuding a heavenly scent.

"Phwaw wassat pong Miss?" Stanley wailed pinching his nose.

"Girlie smells," sniggered William.

"Look!" Adam suddenly shouted, pointing to the square bottle-green pond at the bottom of the terraces. Arriving well before I did, they flung themselves down around the edge and stared down into the dark depths – uncharacteristically and strangely quiet. Stanley then very slowly and imperceptibly nudged William. He put both hands deftly into the water without a ripple and began 'tickling' a huge golden carp. A minute later, out flew the carp in a glorious rainbow orb of tiny iridescent water droplets. It arced in magical slow motion across the dancing sunbeams until the golden fish landed flip-flapping and gasping – right at the feet of a National Trust Warden.

Although the school chose an alternative venue for future outings the visit appears to have had a positive effect on my small group. Adam is now a talented artist, William is a chef, roasting pigs on a pub spit and Stanley relinquished his poaching tendencies to join the other side, becoming a gamekeeper.

Matters of Privacy

"Miss – can I have the key?" whispered Sophie.

The most essential piece of information that the Head had failed to impart when I was first appointed was the children's toilet arrangements.

The boys' toilets were in a stone outbuilding missing its exterior door and thus readily accessible for procrastinating boys. The girls' toilet was a more private affair around the back of the school in a small stone closet. There was no light in there but there were sufficient holes and cracks in the ancient wooden door to allow just enough illumination of the whitewashed walls. It was full of spiders and once housed a hibernating hedgehog amongst the leaves in the corner.

Its musty smell and dim light made it quite spooky and past experiences had made it necessary to allow the girls to attend in pairs as the sticking door often imprisoned the inmates. As the door faced a public footpath it was kept locked with a large black key hung discretely out of reach behind my desk.

So, on that occasion, by the time Sophie had explained what key she wanted and why, it was too late.

School toilets then, as now, could always provide a continuing soap opera of adventures, disasters and scandal. Towards the end of the summer term the Deputy Head marched into my classroom just before morning playtime, announcing, sternly,

"Someone… has done something…IN-APPROPRIATE in the boy's urinal!" The whole class gasped then fell dramatically silent in eager anticipation.

Rosie nudged Anna and whispered.

"What's a pro–pit?"

"Part of the boys' toilet I s'pose." There was a silent pause.

"Where's your eye-nal then?"

" Dunno. Prob'ly something just boys have," and they nodded solemnly.

Suddenly Gary, returning from the toilets and unaware of the Deputy

Head's presence, burst in yelling gleefully,

"There's a gigantic POO in the boys' bogs!"

Hilarity broke the tension. It died down to a contained snigger as the Deputy Head redly remonstrated,

"It is not at all funny, it is a very serious matter. The toilets will now have to be closed AND thoroughly disinfected – but only AFTER the culprit has removed the inappropriate item."

"Ughh!" the girls grimaced.

The Deputy Head continued unabashed.

"The girls may go out and play. The boys will remain until the culprit owns up."

The boys were not unduly upset at missing playtime – this was drama at its best and they wouldn't have missed it for the world. They sat in an expectant huddle keenly glancing around for a guilty crimson face. Then Bobby suddenly put his hand up.

"AH!" gasped the boys accusingly and Bobby's hand shot rapidly down again.

"No! It weren't ME. I was just going to say it might not have been a BOY. It COULD'VE been a girl!"

"Yeah!" they all nodded.

At first there was general agreement on this but after careful consideration they muttered,

"Neh," shaking their heads knowledgably.

The Deputy Head stood patiently silent.

"It could have been a dog," suggested Tony.

"Stew – pid. It couldn't reach", retorted Gary.

"Could've been a giant dog – like an Alsatian!"

"Neh – still couldn't reach."

"A Pony! Paul's got a Pony!"

"Yeh. He's won rosettes an' everything. He's got four red ones – that's FIRSTS Miss!"

Paul was slightly offended by this intimation of guilt and scowled back at Tony.

"I've got a cat. It's called Fluff," piped up Callum.

"Miss! Miss! I've got two Goldfish!"

"I have a Zebra Finch," Edward stated in a superior manner.

"Miss, I've got a rabbit," added Tobias.

Outside the bell rang for end of play and the girls filed back in.

"We WILL discover who did this nasty thing BEFORE you are allowed home for the summer holidays," said the Deputy Head returning to her class.

We never did.

And yes, my boys WERE allowed home for the summer holidays – and so was I.

Postscript

The Beginning of the End

The 1970s were a time of austerity and public cut-backs – especially in education and it soon began to impinge upon the teaching profession. Where there was a slightest hint of a fall in school roll numbers the authorities pounced. Our school numbers now fell five pupils below their designated number for four full-time teachers and on the 'last in first out' rule I was listed for re-deployment within the county. The Head advised me to look for another chosen post before they found me a disagreeable one. The school governors however looked differently upon the situation as did our parents and most other villagers. Their concern was the 'four into three' bulging classes that would remain as a consequence and their other fear was a future closure of their essential village school. Some of them met to discuss a strategy for their 'save our teacher' campaign.

"You must dig your heels in and stay as long as possible."

"They're building more houses in the dairy-land soon, then roll numbers will rise again." The 'soon' turned out to be seven years later.

"Fluff your interviews so you don't get offered anywhere else."

"Your contract is with the school anyway not the county," a more sensible governor informed me. I looked. It was.

I appreciated their support and had no wish to move but also did not want to end up jobless, so I quietly applied for a post in a Church of England school some ten miles away and was invited for a pre-interview

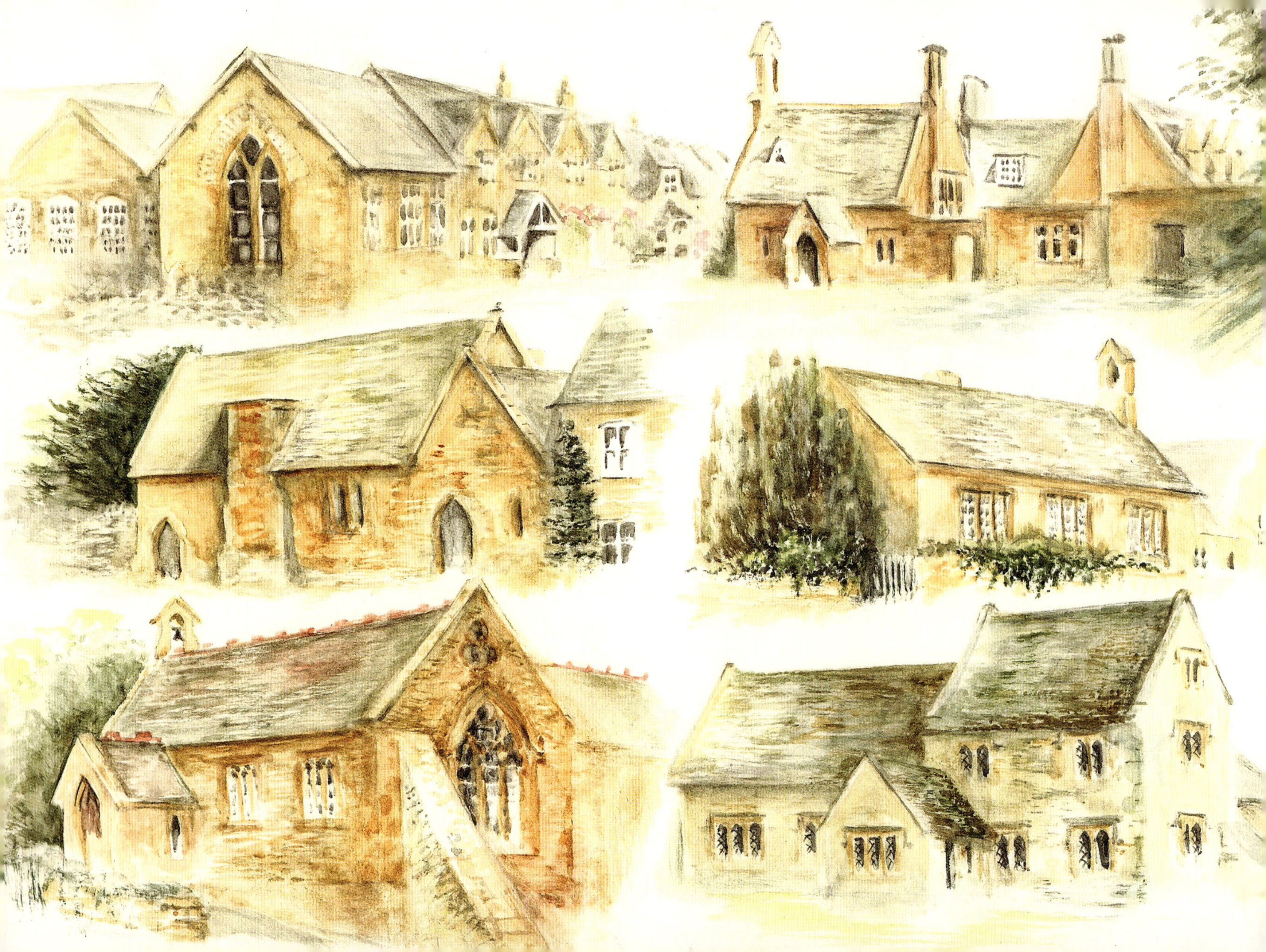

visit. After arriving rather late due to some meanly meandering country lanes I was met at a rusty school gate by a rather irritable Head Teacher who introduced his Chairman of the Governors, the vicar. They led me towards a collection of wartime Nissan huts and asbestos pre-fabs. Inside, they were cold and damp and the gaudy carpets brought in to counteract the cold exuded an unhealthy, musty squelch.

"This was once an emergency war-time secondary school. They moved into a brand new building and now we're waiting for ours," explained the Head with a sideways glance at the vicar.

"Unfortunately," the vicar chirped in cheerfully, "they're expecting the church to 'cough up' half the dosh and our collection box is always half empty."

"Why did you apply for this job – yours is a lovely school?" the Head asked more seriously. As soon as I mentioned redeployment the Head's demeanour changed and he marched silently into his room, closing the door. The abandoned, baffled vicar made polite conversation,

"Would you be able to attend our Sunday Services and boost our little number? We do a very good morning coffee afterwards, with biscuits. Custard Creams."

The Head returned from his room.

"I've withdrawn the job advertisement. I will NOT be told by the County WHO to employ in my own school!" he fumed. I left.

My school governors were delighted when I told them about the job.

"If all Head Teachers do the same, County's strategy won't work!" they all agreed. All except my Head who quietly suggested,

"There's another, much nicer, school you SHOULD have a look at", so I applied again and prepared for the interview.

"Make sure you don't get this one either", said a friend and school governor who popped around for coffee, "Let's find you something completely inappropriate to wear", she said flicking through my wardrobe.

There were seven other candidates at the interview, all newly qualified, full of enthusiasm but from out of the county. Not one of them knew they had wasted their journey under the county's re-deployment rules. The Head and governors went through the long, farcical interview sessions with the seven before calling me in. It was clear by the shiftiness of the panel that the Head had only just told them, after three hours of interviewing, that I had to be their choice, unless I was totally unsuitable. Now their backs were up and they were poised for battle.

"What makes you think YOU, above all those others, are the most suitable for our school?" one asked incredulously and before I had time to answer,

"What do you know about the Warnock Report – just published last week?" another governor asked, leaning forwards to almost touch my nose.

"To be fair," interrupted the Head, "That Report has only just been published and …"

"No!" the governor bawled banging his hand on the table, "it's a perfectly fair question. It's about teaching Special Needs children in

Mainstream Schools and SHE ..." he pointed "... might be teaching MY Special Needs child here. Do you have any experience of Autism Spectrum Disorder or Down's Syndrome ... hey?"

"Well, not yet," I muttered.

"That's that then, you won't be able to work here will you?" and he slammed down his notes and sat back in his chair. A slightly more genteel questioner asked me if I had any interests outside teaching. Anxious to rectify my previous disastrous answer I reeled off a list of activities for each evening and every weekend hoping to impress them with my versatility and boundless energy.

They said they would let me know.

The following day I was called in to see my Head.

"I've just had a phone call from my colleague about your interview. Frankly I'm very disappointed in you. I went to a lot of trouble to find you that job and what do I hear? I hear that you told them you had no experience whatsoever with Special Needs children and you were so busy with your own interests you'd be unable to attend any after-school functions. In the light of that they cannot employ you. Instead, they are re-organising their classes with two part-timers," he sniffed.

Chastised like a child, I left the Head Teacher's room. I remained on the re-deployment list as cost-cutting cut severely into our small school and demoralised staff moved on. The Head left teaching altogether and went to live by the sea and the Deputy Head took early retirement. A new head was appointed who brought her own two staff with her and our four cosy classes were reconstituted into three over-flowing ones.

I was subsequently offered a job in the school where my disastrous interview took place. I'd certainly have a lot to prove there!

Little Green Shoots Illustrations

How to buy prints

To purchase prints of any of the illustrations, or a compilation, please contact me at: Jennys.art@hotmail.co.uk where I can discuss your order personally – Jenny Henderson.

A Village School	Front Cover		Page		Page		Page
	Page	An Autumn Drive	22	Primroses	43	A Speckled Hen	63
Red Admirals	1	The Football Game	23	The Boys' Playground	44	Fox Face	63
The Pink Dress	2	My Big Green Tractor	24	Daffodil	46	A Cottage Garden	64
A Village School	3	My Little Green Bike	25	Cows at Pasture	47	Portrait of a Hereford	65
Jack and Russell	4	The Lesson	26	The Games Hut	48	Fallen Flowers	66
Bird-watching	5	Wax Crayons	27	A Classroom Scene	49	The Maypole	67
Bonfire on the Green	6	Candlelight	29	A Gerbil	49	Kittens	68
School Time	7	The Carol Concert	30	Frog	50	Hedgerow in May	69
		Christmas Post	31	Trot-on!	51	Pond Dipping	70
AUTUMN TERM				The Troublesome Trio	52	Yellow Fridge with	71
Autumn Amble	8	**SPRING TERM**		Whoa!	53	Geraniums – Still Life	
The School Door	9	Home in the Snow	32	A Fluffy Chick	54	The Limes	73
The Egg Basket	11	The Snowy Road	33	Painted Eggs	54	Straw Hat	73
The Kitchen Window	12	The Ice Slide	34	Willows and Geese	55	Cap	73
Conkers	13	When Icicles Hang	35			A Peacock Butterfly	74
A Village Shop	14	Boy and Rabbit	36	**SUMMER TERM**		The Golden Carp	75
The Little Blue Mini	15	Snowdrop Cottage	37	The Hay Meadow	56	Blue Doors	76
Goldfinches	16	Tip-up	38	Cricket Ball	57	Kingfisher	77
School with Ivy	16	The Black Lab	38	Bean Bag Bucket	57	Meadowsweet	78/79
The Field Mice	17	Cat in the Bin	39	A Cool Head	58		
A Ginger Cat	18	Cat and Kitten	39	The School Bell	59	School Sketches	80
A Cotswold Farm	18/19	Tip	40	Tennis Ball	59	Little Green Shoots	82
Freshly Farrowed	20	A Cow in the Kitchen	41	Cricket	61	Butterflies and Berries	84
The Old School	21	Tadpoles	42	Playground Pals	62	The Watermill	Back Cover

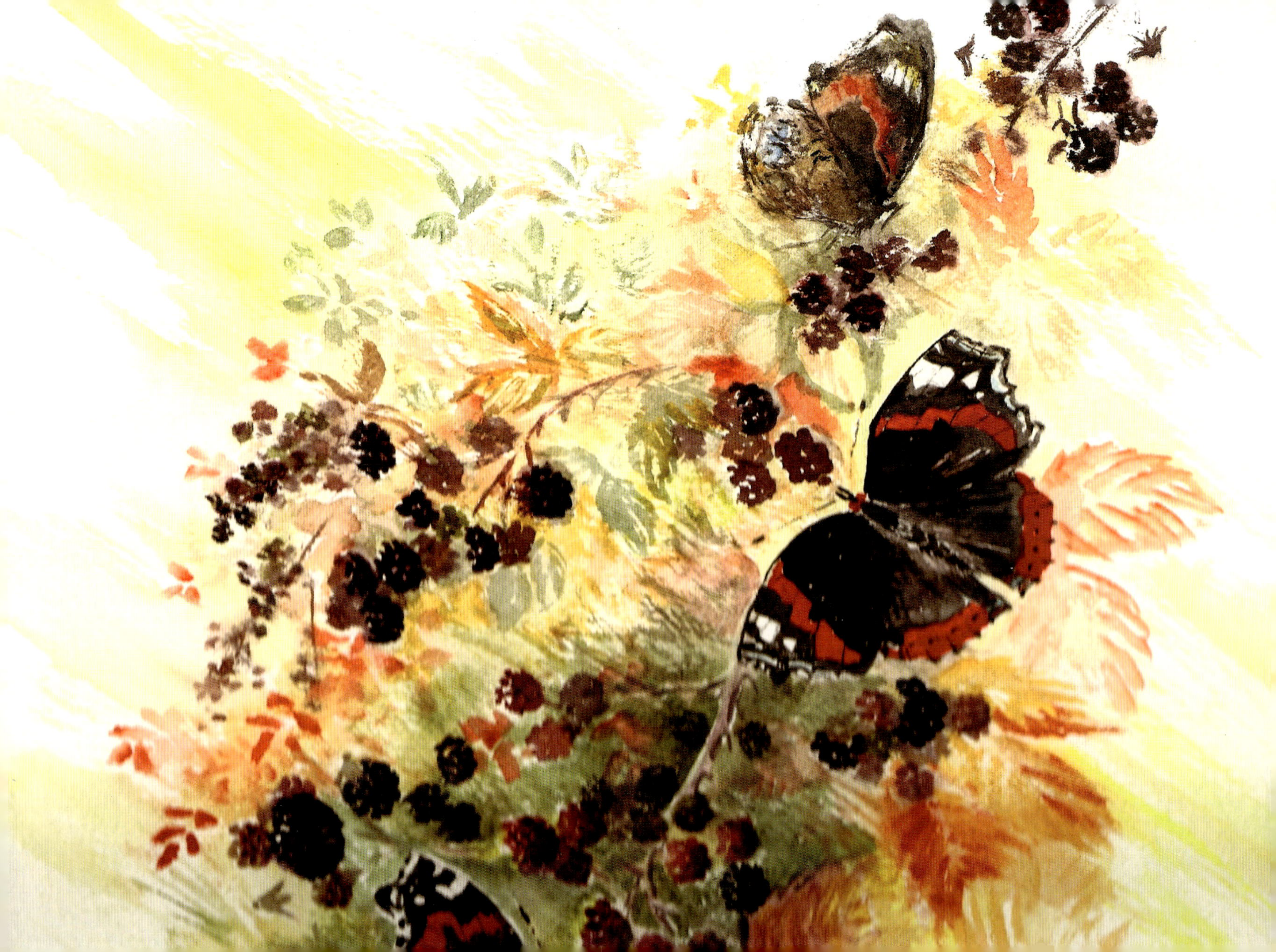